# WATERLOO TO
# WEST COUNTRY

## A journey from London to Penzance
## during the days of steam

### IAN BEARDSLEY & RHYS JONES

Published by Platform 5 Publishing Ltd,
52 Broadfield Road, Sheffield, S8 0XJ. England.

Printed in England by The Amadeus Press, Cleckheaton, West Yorkshire.

ISBN: 978 1 909431 94 2

**Front cover top:** The introduction of new diesel-hydraulic locomotives and diesel multiple units (DMUs) during the late 1950s and 1960s saw off the remaining steam traction from the Western Region, which changed the railway scene dramatically. With only a matter of years to go until it was withdrawn from service, ex-Great Western Railway (GWR) Collett 4900 Class 4-6-0 No. 4948 "Northwick Hall" heads westwards through Dawlish with a Class B stopping passenger service on 19 September 1959. *Dave Marriot*

**Front cover bottom:** In what would have been an almost everyday sight at the time, rebuilt Bulleid Merchant Navy Class 4-6-2 No. 35014 "Nederland Line" leads the "Atlantic Coast Express" through Farnborough on 6 September 1962. Within just a couple of years, however, the service, which directly linked Waterloo with various seaside destinations in the West Country, was withdrawn. The locomotive survived a little longer, but the continued modernisation of the British Railways (BR) network through the 1960s meant that scenes such as this were soon nothing more than a distant memory, with steam traction being completely eradicated from the Southern Region by 9 July 1967. *Dave Marriot*

**Back cover:** As well as the withdrawal of BR's remaining steam locomotives, the 1960s saw numerous lines closed in an effort to cut costs. One such route was that to the west of Wadebridge, which continued alongside the Camel Estuary to the fishing port of Padstow. Now part of the popular Camel Trail, this was officially closed on 30 January 1967 after passenger services over the line from Bodmin Road were withdrawn, services over the North Cornwall Line (from Halwill Junction) having ceased in the October of the previous year. An unidentified Collett 4575 Class 2-6-2T accelerates a Bodmin-bound service away from Wadebridge on 13 June 1960. *Dave Marriot*

**Title page:** Far away from the hustle and bustle of the London suburbs where it used to work, ex-London & South Western Railway (LSWR) Beattie 0298 Class 2-4-0WT No. 30585 passes Dunmere Junction with a short freight train on 15 June 1960. Situated on the outskirts of Bodmin, this was where the branch from the china clay dries at Wenfordbridge left the line to Bodmin North. Although this might not seem like an obvious location for a railway photographer to frequent, with relatively little by way of traffic to record, this part of the country was the only place that the venerable Beattie Well Tanks could be found in their latter days of service, which ensured its popularity with enthusiasts. *Dave Marriot*

# ■ CONTENTS

# ■ INTRODUCTION

**Above:** Rebuilt Bulleid West Country Class 4-6-2 No. 34008 "Padstow" and an unidentified BR Standard Class 4MT 2-6-0 are seen stabled at Nine Elms motive power depot on 18 June 1967, just three weeks before the end of steam on the Southern Region. *Rhys Jones*

For many rail enthusiasts, it is the ever-changing nature of the railway scene that helps to maintain their interest in it. Infrastructure, operating practices, rolling stock and even routes themselves have changed significantly over the years, particularly so in the South-West of England. As well as the replacement of the remaining steam locomotives with diesel traction, the former LSWR main line to Exeter was heavily rationalised westwards of Salisbury during the 1960s as BR sought to balance the books in the face of decreasing ridership. Stations, goods yards and motive power depots were shut, lengthy sections of track were singled, and some of the branch lines that once carried holidaymakers to seaside destinations such as Lyme Regis, Seaton and Sidmouth were wiped off the rail map altogether. It was a similar situation in the north of Devon and Cornwall, with the increasing usage of motor cars resulting in the closure of not only various lightly used branches but also most of the ex-LSWR lines west of Exeter, including the main line to Plymouth via Okehampton and the North Cornwall Line. Fortunately, through photographic collections such as that belonging to Rhys Jones, we can look back on what has been lost and over the following pages the reader will be taken on a journey from Waterloo to the West Country during the latter days of steam.

Having been bought a Kodak Brownie 127 by his grandmother for passing his 11+ exams, Rhys has been a keen railway photographer since the age of 12 and continues to be a regular contributor to the railway press. Despite being based in North Wales until a move to Sheffield in 1968, he managed to record something of the final years of steam on BR's Southern Region himself. By then, his "Box Brownie" had been replaced with an Agfa Silette, which had a maximum shutter speed of 1/125th of a second – a considerable improvement over the 1/60th of a second maximum offered by his earlier equipment, but still not enough to stop anything travelling at speed. As such, ahead of his first All Line rail rover, aged about 16, Rhys assumed control of his father's Kodak Retinette 1B. Although this still had to be manually focussed, it had a much-improved maximum shutter speed of 1/500th of a second. Even so, unlike with today's digital cameras, he had to be quite selective about what he photographed, and the results were often more down to luck that judgement! These photos are therefore supplemented by those of his close friends, Derek Penney and the late Alfred David Marriot (Dave), who were part of a group of Sheffield-based schoolboy locomotive spotters turned photographers, which also included the late Keith Pirt. Between them they built up an extensive archive of scenes from southern and south-west England in the late 1950s and 1960s, a small selection of which appear on the following pages.

Born in Sheffield in 1935, Dave's photographic activities began with the use of a simple folding camera using black and white

**Below:** Seen during the same visit to Nine Elms as illustrated earlier, rebuilt Bulleid Merchant Navy Class 4-6-2 No. 35030 "Elder-Dempster Lines" is pictured at rest on the south London depot. Despite various parts of its valve gear having been removed, the locomotive would go on to work the Southern Region's final steam-hauled passenger train three weeks later, the 14.09 Weymouth–Waterloo on 9 July 1967. It was one of seven Merchant Navy Class locomotives in service that day, the others being Nos. 35003 "Royal Mail", 35007 "Aberdeen Commonwealth", 35008 "Orient Line", 35013 "Blue Funnel", 35023 "Holland-Afrika Line" and 35028 "Clan Line". This claim to fame was not enough to ensure its survival into preservation, however. The locomotive was scrapped by J Buttigieg of Newport, Monmouthshire in December 1968. *Rhys Jones*

film on visits to motive power depots, which he often made with the local branch of the Railway Correspondence & Travel Society (RCTS). Work, as an apprentice cabinet maker, gradually gave rise to better cameras becoming more affordable, and his interest turned to photographing moving trains, this eventually becoming the main focus of his hobby activities. He took up colour photography in the late 1950s, but this was almost immediately interrupted by National Service with the army, mostly abroad. The change to colour also meant a change to 35 mm format and another succession of cameras leading eventually to a Leica M3, with which his most satisfying work was done. Following the demise of steam, Dave's interest in railways waned for a while, but his photographic activities restarted with new friends and he eventually embraced the world of digital photography, continuing to record the changing scene until he was prevented from doing so by the onset of ill health. Sadly, he passed away in 2020, with his final years being spent in a nursing home.

**Above:** Rebuilt Bulleid Merchant Navy Class 4-6-2 No. 35022 "Holland America Line" awaits its departure from the terminus with a westbound express in the summer of 1964. An unidentified electric multiple unit (EMU) can be seen in the background. *Derek Penney*

**Left:** In a scene that would have probably been overlooked by many photographers who wished to save their film for something more interesting, such as a Bulleid Pacific, Maunsell U Class 2-6-0 No. 31803 passes Farnborough with a lengthy train of ballast hopper wagons in tow on 13 July 1964. *Dave Marriot*

Although both Dave and Derek possessed lineside passes, limited finances and a large reliance on public transport meant that they were unable to exploit these fully. As such, some parts of the route were not covered in as greater detail as others; some, such as Andover, were overlooked altogether. A number of these gaps have, however, been filled using Rhys' more recent shots of railtours recreating the days of steam. We hope that we have therefore been successful in giving the reader a good impression of what it was like to make a journey from Waterloo to the South-West during those halcyon days the late 1950s and early 1960s, and that we can sufficiently whet your appetite for the volumes to follow, which will focus on other parts of the country.

# CHAPTER I
## THE SOUTH WESTERN MAIN LINE: FROM WATERLOO TO WORTING JUNCTION

Our journey begins at Waterloo, which was the central London terminus of the LSWR. It was never intended to be a terminus, however. Upon its opening in 1848, it was planned that the line would be extended further towards the City of London. As such, for much of the 19th century the LSWR was reluctant to provide Waterloo with the facilities that would be expected of a grand terminus and the station was developed in a haphazard manner to cope with rising passenger demand. After its plans to extend the line into the City were twice rejected, a deep-level underground railway was instead built to connect Waterloo with Bank. With the long-desired commuter service provided by the Waterloo & City Railway, the LSWR eventually opted to totally rebuild the station in a project known as the "Grand Transformation". The new station, which consisted of 21 platforms, a 700 ft-long concourse and an office block built in the Imperial Baroque style out of Portland stone, was opened in stages from 1909 to 1922, its construction having continued sporadically throughout World War I. It was formally opened on 21 March 1922 by HM Queen Mary. During the station's rebuilding, in October 1915 the LSWR introduced 600 V DC third rail electric services onto the route from Waterloo to Wimbledon via East Putney. Electrification gradually spread to further routes over the years that followed, including the Hounslow Loop and the lines to Hampton Court and Shepperton in 1916, but apart from the installation of a public address system by the Southern Railway (SR), the LSWR's successor, in the early 1930s and some alterations to the signalling and track layout to improve the station's approaches later that same decade, Waterloo remained largely unchanged for many years. In fact, it was the last London terminus to have steam-hauled services, these continuing until 9 July 1967, after which trains to and from and Bournemouth were formed from EMUs, with Birmingham Railway Carriage & Wagon Type 3 diesel locomotives (Class 33s) fitted with push-pull equipment being used to work the trains beyond Bournemouth (to and from Weymouth).

From Waterloo, we take the South Western Main Line as far as Worting Junction, a distance of just over 50 miles. Shared by services to Southampton and destinations along the Dorset coast, the route, most of which was opened in the late 1830s under the auspices of the London & Southampton Railway – the forerunner of the LSWR, runs through the south-western suburbs of the capital, passing the line's former terminus and site of the LSWR's Locomotive, Carriage and Wagons Works (and the main motive power depot for services over the South Western Main Line) at Nine Elms, through Vauxhall, Clapham Junction, Earlsfield, Wimbledon and numerous other suburban stations (shown on the accompanying map) before heading into Surrey. Its gradients are relatively gentle, although after passing the former racetrack at Brooklands westbound trains face a climb of around 1 in 300 for ten miles from Byfleet & New Haw, which during steam days enabled some sustained high-speed running in the opposite direction, with Bulleid Pacifics being recorded at speeds in excess of 100 mph on multiple occasions towards the end of steam. The long level stretches, particularly those beyond what was then the outer extremity of the commuter belt, were also conducive to this. Until 1967, the 750 V DC third rail electrification, which gradually replaced the 600 V DC system to become standard across the whole of the electrified network in the southern counties, came to an end at Pirbright Junction, where the Alton line veers away to the south. From there, the line passes through an area of pine-clad heathlands, but its surroundings become increasingly built-up as it nears Farnborough, Fleet and Basingstoke.

### Basingstoke

Basingstoke is the first major station along our route beyond what was then the limit of electrification. At its eastern end there are carriage sidings on either side of the line, flanked by shallow cuttings through the chalklands of north Hampshire, and just after these the former GWR line from Reading trails in on the right. This was for the first eight years of its existence, until 1856, a broad gauge line. It had no connection to the adjacent LSWR line, a separate station being provided to the north of its competitor's. A transfer shed with broad gauge track on the north side and standard gauge on the south enabled goods to be exchanged between the two systems. This laborious arrangement became superfluous when the route was converted to mixed gauge, which also enabled the operation of through services to and from the Midlands and North of England via Oxford. No longer required, the GWR station was eventually closed in 1932, after which its services used the neighbouring facilities of the SR. The former GWR engine shed was likewise dispensed with in 1950, it being demolished to make way for more sidings. That at the opposite end of the station, which was built by the LSWR in the early 1900s, remained open until March 1963. After this it acted as a servicing point until the end of Southern Region steam in July 1967. It was demolished two years later. As well as the three-road engine shed, there was a goods yard at the western end of the station and slightly further on from this the route of the Basingstoke & Alton Light Railway diverged to the south. Closed as a through route in 1936, a short stub remained in situ until 1967 to serve the Thornycroft vehicle factory.

Worting Junction, where we leave the South Western Main Line, is three miles west of Basingstoke. It is surrounded by farmland, which dominates the next part of our route through the North Hampshire Downs and along the southern edge of Salisbury Plain. Originally a flat junction, this became a problem as the volume of traffic and the number of conflicting movements increased. In order to alleviate the bottleneck, in the late 1890s the LSWR built the Battledown Flyover, which carries the Up line from Southampton over the lines to and from Salisbury on a lattice girder bridge. In addition to this, the formation on the north side of the line was widened so that dedicated tracks could be provided for each of the two routes, the outer ones being for trains to and from Southampton and the inner pair for trains to and from Salisbury.

# THE SOUTH WEST MAIN LINE AND ITS CONNECTIONS

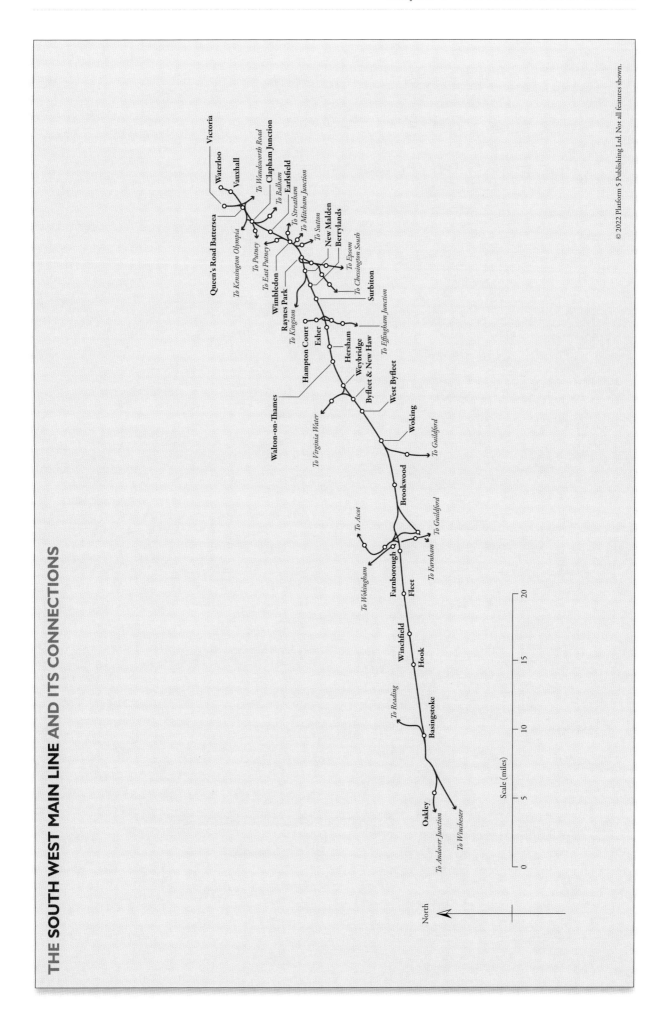

**Right:** In this undated view from the summer of 1964, rebuilt Bulleid Merchant Navy Class 4-6-2 No. 35022 "Holland America Line", flanked by BR Standard Class 4MT 2-6-4T No. 80095 and an unidentified Light Pacific, awaits its departure from Waterloo with what is believed to be the "Atlantic Coast Express".

Intended as a way of promoting its services to and from the South-West of England, the "Atlantic Coast Express", or the "ACE" as it was affectionately known, was a titled train introduced by the SR in July 1926. Its name was the result of a staff competition, the winning entry being submitted by Mr F Rowland, a guard from Woking, who was awarded a prize of three guineas. As its title suggests, the train served various destinations on the north coasts of Devon and Cornwall, including Ilfracombe, Bideford, Bude and Padstow, which at about 260 miles from Waterloo was the most westerly outpost of the SR. It also included portions for Plymouth and coastal destinations in east Devon, including Sidmouth and Exmouth. The heavy reliance on holiday traffic meant that the train changed with the seasons. During the summer months, the number of passengers wishing to travel on the "ACE" was such that a second train had to be provided in each direction, while on summer Saturdays as many as five or six would be needed to cope. By comparison, only one train was needed in winter, with this stopping several times en route for coaches to be detached, which meant it was far from express. But for a brief pause during World War II, the train continued to operate until the 1960s, by which time increasing car ownership was eroding passenger numbers. The service ceased running at the start of September 1964 after the lines west of Salisbury were transferred to BR's Western Region.

Despite them being designed as mixed-traffic locomotives, or so O V S Bulleid (the SR's Chief Mechanical Engineer at the time) said in order for their construction to be signed off during wartime, when what little money was available was supposed to have been put towards locomotives and rolling stock that would support the war effort, No. 35022 and its classmates were for many years a regular sight on express passenger services between Waterloo and Exeter, the Merchant Navies having taken over this leg of the "ACE" when it was reintroduced after the war. Weight restrictions prevented the locomotives from travelling beyond Exeter, however. Westwards of there, its portions were generally handled by the lighter Battle of Britain or West Country Class Pacifics, although other locomotives were used on occasions.

No. 35022 was outshopped from Eastleigh Works in October 1948 and was at first based at Exmouth Junction motive power depot. It was named on 24 January 1949 in a joint ceremony with No. 35023 "Holland-Afrika Line" at Southampton Docks by Mr W H de Moncy, who was then the Managing Director of the shipping line. With the intention of improving the economy and performance of the class, between March 1952 and January 1954 the locomotive was involved in various tests at the newly developed locomotive testing station at Rugby. It was also used in a series of controlled road trials over the Settle and Carlisle Line during this time. It was concluded from these experiments that the locomotive was an inconsistent performer, although it was recognised that there was room for improvement with its draughting and the steam-operated reversing gear, which was one of a number of novel features of the design. Mechanically, there were no reported issues other than one of its coupling rods buckling in a slip at speed on the test plant rollers. Such problems were not unusual across the class, with stories coming from shed staff that the locomotives' coupling rods sometimes had to be straightened out using jacks placed against shed walls. As well as this, it was discovered in April 1953 that there was a problem with the design of the crank axle on the locomotives, with No. 35020 "Bibby Line" being partially derailed after suffering a crank axle failure at Crewkerne. This incident, which some sources say was caused by corrosion at the base of the chain sprocket, led to the crank axle on the locomotives being redesigned; it also alerted BR's management to the need for the class to be rebuilt to ease maintenance and eliminate the various deficiencies in the design, including the chain-driven valve gear and the oil bath in which it was located, the mechanical lubricators, the reversing gear and the drawbar between a locomotive and its tender. The distinctive air-smoothed casing would also be removed as part of the rebuilding, which was overseen by R G Jarvis – then the Southern Region's Chief Technical Assistant (Locomotives), giving the locomotives a more conventional appearance.

No. 35022 was rebuilt at Eastleigh Works in June 1956, two years after being transferred to Bournemouth motive power depot and by which point it had covered some 329 083 miles. It remained at Bournemouth until March 1960, being used to haul heavy trains such as the "Bournemouth Belle" to and from the Capital. Then, in March 1960, it returned to Exmouth Junction for a further stay of almost four years, eventually moving to Nine Elms (where the locomotive was based at the time of this photograph being taken) in February 1964. After accumulating 903 542 miles in service, the locomotive was withdrawn from Weymouth shed (where it had been based since September 1964) in May 1966 and was subsequently sold to Woodham Brothers Ltd of Barry for disposal. As with many other locomotives that ended up at the South Wales scrapyard, it survived, however, being sold into preservation in 1983 and moving to the fledgling Swanage Railway under the care of the Southern Steam Trust in 1986. It has since had several owners but at the time of writing had yet to be restored. *Derek Penney*

**Right:** Ex-SR Bulleid West Country Class 4-6-2 No. 34023 "Blackmore Vale" rests in the gloom of what is thought to be the "Old Shed" at Nine Elms motive power depot during the early hours of 18 June 1967. The locomotive, which was built at Brighton Works in February 1946 as part of Order No. 2561, would be withdrawn within a matter of weeks of this photograph being taken (upon the end of Southern Region steam in July 1967). It accumulated a total of 921 268 miles during its 21 years of service, much of which would have been while travelling between Waterloo and the West of England, the locomotive having spent most of its life based at locations along this route. Allocated from new to Ramsgate motive power depot, it was transferred to Nine Elms in July 1947. It then went to Salisbury in February 1950, being based there until a move to Exmouth Junction in May 1951. It remained at Exmouth Junction until September 1964, after which it was based at Eastleigh almost until the end of its career. Its final few months of service, from April to July 1967, were spent at Nine Elms, which was the depot responsible for providing locomotives for services in and out of the nearby Waterloo station. Located on the southern side of the South Western Main Line, the expansive depot was demolished shortly after the end of Southern Region steam to make way for the construction of New Covent Garden Market. *Rhys Jones*

**Right:** Taken from a passing train, ex-LSWR Urie H16 Class 4-6-2T No. 30520 is pictured on a rake of empty coaching stock just outside of Waterloo on 9 September 1962. Along with three of its four classmates, Nos. 30516, 30518 and 30519, the locomotive, which was originally designed to work cross-London freight trains, was withdrawn just two months later. No. 30517 remained in service until December that year. All except No. 30518 were disposed of during 1963. *Derek Penney*

**Below:** Rebuilt Bulleid Merchant Navy Class 4-6-2 No. 35029 "Ellerman Lines" heads a Down West of England express through Clapham in September 1964. The penultimate member of the class to be built, No. 35029 entered service at Bournemouth motive power depot in February 1949 but was transferred to Dover eight months later to work boat trains to and from Victoria. Having had its original malachite green livery replaced with BR express blue in January 1951, the locomotive was named on 1 March that year at Southampton Docks by Mr A F Hull, who was then the Chairman of the shipping company after which it was named. It was, in fact, the last member of the class to be named. Following a further repaint, into BR green, in July 1952, the locomotive was reallocated to Nine Elms in June 1958 and, after covering 428 621 miles, it was rebuilt at Eastleigh Works in September 1959. Having been moved away from Nine Elms in September 1964, the locomotive was withdrawn from service with a total mileage of 748 343, which was the lowest of all the class, at Weymouth depot in September 1966. It was subsequently sold to Woodham Brothers Ltd of Barry but was resold by the scrap merchants and is now part of the National Collection on display at the National Railway Museum in York. It owes its survival not to any historical or technical significance but the decision that the museum should have a sectioned steam locomotive for educational purposes. *Derek Penney*

**Above right:** No. 34008 "Padstow" leads a Bournemouth-bound train consisting mostly of maroon-liveried BR Mark 1 coaches through the cutting at Earlsfield in September 1964.

One of the first of Bulleid's Light Pacific locomotives, which were outwardly similar to the earlier Merchant Navies and incorporated many of their innovative features but were designed to be lighter so that they could be used over a wider variety of routes – particularly in the South-West of England and around the Kent coast, the locomotive was built under Order No. 2561 and was outshopped from Brighton Works in September 1945. Allocated from new to Exmouth Junction motive power depot, it was initially referred to as No. 21C108, Bulleid having adopted a Continental practice whereby letters and numbers were used to describe locomotives. The first two digits referred to the number of unpowered leading and trailing axles, the letter indicated the number of coupled driving axles, while the final digit(s) represented the engine's number. This scheme was later abolished by BR, however, with the locomotive, which had by then been named "Padstow", becoming No. 34008 in April 1949.

The first 48 of the Light Pacifics, Nos. 21C101–21C148 (later 34001–34048), were named after cities, towns, villages and geographical features in the West of England that were either served by or situated near to the SR's routes, with what became No. 34008 being named by L H L Saunders, the then Chairman of Padstow Urban District Council, in a ceremony at Padstow station on 31 October 1945. In addition to its nameplates, the locomotive was fitted with plaques bearing the Arms of the Duchy of Cornwall and West Country Class scrolls beneath these. Its classmates were similarly given the coat of arms connected with the location after which they were named. Not all the West Countries carried these plaques, however. As names relating to the West of England would have meant little to the residents of the South-East, the management of the SR decided that some of the later locomotives (Nos. 21C149–21C170, 34071–34090, 34109 and 34110) were to be named after aircraft, airfields, commanders and squadrons associated with the Battle of Britain, with their names being selected from a list of suggestions supplied by the Royal Air Force's Head of Public Relations. These locomotives were duly referred to as the Battle of Britain Class, but other than their wing-shaped nameplates they were no different to the West Country Class locomotives. All except the last of the locomotives was also given vitreous enamelled plaques depicting the badge or crest most appropriate to their name. Why No. 34110 did not receive its plaques is unclear. Some sources suggest that their manufacturer had retired by the time that the locomotive was complete, although others state that they were for some unknown reason left in storage at Eastleigh Works.

After its renumbering, No. 34008 was transferred from Exmouth Junction to Nine Elms in March 1951. It remained at the south London shed until September 1958, after which it was allocated to Brighton. By this point, with the West Countries and Battle of

Britains suffering similar problems to the Merchant Navies, the locomotives had started to be rebuilt to R G Jarvis' revised design, which resulted in their nameplates being repositioned above the running plate as illustrated. No. 34008's rebuilding took place at Eastleigh Works during July 1960. Not all the Light Pacifics were rebuilt, however. With the locomotives being relatively new and end of steam in sight, it was difficult to justify the costs of doing so, meaning that 50 of the locomotives remained unrebuilt.

Having been based at Eastleigh from September 1962 to June 1966, No. 34008 was eventually withdrawn from service at Nine Elms in June 1967. It covered a total of 961 734 miles during its career. The locomotive was scrapped by J Buttigieg of Newport, Monmouthshire between October 1967 and February 1968. *Derek Penney*

**Above right:** A close-up of the wing-shaped nameplate and, below it, the plaque carried by preserved Bulleid Battle of Britain Class 4-6-2 No. 34072 "257 Squadron". In the case of this locomotive, the plaque depicts the squadron's badge, which features the Burmese Chinthe at its centre and around it the squadron's motto, "Thay Myay Gyee Shin Shwe Hti", which translates as "Death or Glory". *Rhys Jones*

**Above:** The black-backed nameplate of ex-SR Bulleid West Country Class 4-6-2 No. 34046 "Braunton" and, above it, the plaque bearing the Devonian village's crest that was added in preservation. Note that as "Braunton" was one of the locomotives that was rebuilt under R G Jarvis its nameplates are mounted on the running plates rather than the side of the air-smoothed casing as they were originally. The Light Pacifics' nameplates were painted in various colours during their careers, with those on the West Country Class locomotives appearing either in red or black. Those on the Battle of Britains were similarly treated for a time, but many were painted in sky blue. *Rhys Jones*

**Above:** Rebuilt Bulleid Merchant Navy Class 4-6-2 No. 35017 "Belgian Marine" is pictured near Earlsfield in September 1964 whilst working "The Royal Wessex" towards Waterloo.

One of the lessor-known titled trains, "The Royal Wessex" was an express service connecting Waterloo with Bournemouth, Swanage and Weymouth. The name was introduced by BR's Southern Region in May 1951 in connection with the Festival of Britain that year, although the origins of the service itself can be traced back to the days of the LSWR, which began operating non-stop services between Waterloo and Bournemouth in 1911. By the 1960s, "The Royal Wessex" had become the heaviest train to regularly operate on the Bournemouth line, often being made up of as many 13 coaches. With the increased weight of the train, plus additional station stops at Winchester, Southampton and Brockenhurst, the schedule was a lot more demanding than in the LSWR era and gave rise to some impressive performances from the Merchant Navy Class locomotives, which were the rostered traction.

Built at Eastleigh Works, the locomotive entered traffic as No. 21C17 at Nine Elms in April 1945 wearing wartime black livery. Having been repainted into malachite green in October 1945, it was named at Victoria station on 22 November that year by Monsieur G Rongvaux, who was then the Belgian Minister of Communications. In April 1948, the locomotive was renumbered as No. 35017, and in preparation for its participation in the locomotive exchanges the following month it was paired with a London, Midland & Scottish Railway (LMS) 4000 gallon tender, which enabled its water supplies to be replenished on the move (there were no water troughs on the Southern Region, so the tender that was usually coupled to the locomotive was not equipped with a water scoop). During these trials, the locomotive was tested on the East Coast Main Line between King's Cross and Leeds and also on the West Coast Main Line between Euston and Carlisle. Once they were over, it regained its original tender in June 1948. The locomotive was repainted into BR express blue in July the following year, then into BR green in April 1953. After covering 594 522 miles, it was rebuilt at Eastleigh Works in March 1957. The locomotive was eventually withdrawn from service at Weymouth, where it had been based since September 1964, in July 1966, having accumulated a total of 1 017 754 miles. It was scrapped by J Buttigieg, Newport, Monmouthshire in September that year. *Derek Penney*

**Below:** Rebuilt Bulleid Merchant Navy Class 4-6-2 No. 35026 "Lamport & Holt Line" leads the 10.00 departure from Waterloo for the West Country through the cutting at Earlsfield in early September 1964. Judging by the first coach at least, the train appears to be well loaded, but it will be well within the capabilities of the powerful locomotive.

Built as part of the third and final order for Merchant Navies to be placed with Eastleigh Works, Order No. 3393, No. 35026 entered service at Bournemouth motive power depot in December 1948. Within just a matter of months its unlined malachite green livery was replaced by a coat of BR express blue and by March 1950 the locomotive had been transferred to Stewarts Lane, where it was based until January 1957. Its naming came on 15 January 1951, it being named in a joint ceremony with No. 35028 by Mr S H Mercer, the London manager of Lamport & Holt Line, at Southampton Docks. After being repainted into BR green livery in June 1952, the locomotive led a relatively uneventful life until it was admitted to Eastleigh Works for rebuilding into the condition in which it is illustrated here, by which point it travelled some 311 063 miles (the AWS equipment and speedometer were later additions, however). Upon its release from the works, in January 1957, the locomotive was reallocated to Exmouth Junction, but it was not to stay there for long. By May 1957 it had been transferred back to Bournemouth to work services over the route between Weymouth and Waterloo. It was returned to Exmouth Junction in April 1959 and remained there until February 1964, by which point the shed had been taken over by the Western Region. Upon its transfer back to the Southern Region it was allocated to Nine Elms, staying there until being transferred to Weymouth shortly after this photograph was taken. Its withdrawal came in March 1967, it having amounted 858 784 miles during its 18 years of service. Having been sold to John Cashmore Ltd of Newport, Monmouthshire, the locomotive was scrapped in September 1967.

Headquartered in Liverpool, the shipping line after which the locomotive was named was founded in 1845 and was initially concerned with the transportation of Egyptian cotton used in the Lancashire mills, but it quickly grew to also serve destinations in India, New Zealand, Australia and North and South America. In 1865, it founded the Liverpool, Brazil & River Plate Steam Navigation Co Ltd to operate steam ships out of Antwerp, Glasgow, Liverpool and London, and in later years this company became the first to ferry coffee from Brazil to New York using iron-hulled ships, disproving the theory that an iron hull would taint the flavour of the coffee. In doing so the company established a successful triangular trade taking manufactured goods from the UK to Brazil, coffee from Brazil to the US and raw materials, such as wheat, from the US to the UK. Having subsequently won contacts to carry mail from Belgium to Brazil, Uruguay and Argentina and established further services in South America, additional subsidiaries were set up, and by 1890 the company's fleet reached a peak of 59 ships. After being made a limited company in 1911, Lamport & Holt was taken over by its nearest rival, the Royal Mail Steam Packet Company, but the sinking of SS Vestris in November 1928, the Wall Street crash in 1929 and the company's Chairman, Lord Kylsant, being tried for misrepresenting the state of its affairs resulted in trade being all but wiped out and the company collapsed. It was reconstituted in 1932, under the leadership of a new Chair, as Royal Mail Lines, with Lamport & Holt becoming Lamport & Holt Line Ltd. Having diversified into cruises during the slump in global trade, the new company was eventually sold to Vestey Group (owner of Blue Star Line) in 1944. The Lamport & Holt name continued to be used until the early 1990s, after which the Vestey Group's remaining trade with South America was undertaken by Blue Star. *Derek Penney*

**Right:** Rebuilt Bulleid Merchant Navy Class 4-6-2 No. 35024 "East Asiatic Company" speeds through Wimbledon with a Down West of England express in September 1964.

Built at Eastleigh Works as one of the final batch of the 30-strong fleet, the locomotive entered traffic at Exmouth Junction in November 1948. At first it carried an unlined malachite green livery but in February 1949 became the first member of the class to be painted into BR express blue, its red bands being replaced with black and white lining the following month. It was named in a ceremony at Waterloo station on 5 May 1949 by HRH Prince Axel of Denmark, who was then the Chairman of the shipping line after which the locomotive was named. In May 1951, it was repainted once again, this time into BR green, it again being the first of the class to be so treated. Rebuilt at Eastleigh Works in April 1959 after accumulating 552 053 miles, the locomotive was then transferred to Bournemouth before being moved to Nine Elms in January 1962 and Weymouth in September 1964. Its withdrawal came in January 1965, by which point the locomotive had travelled 839 415 miles. It was scrapped by Ivor C Woodfield & Sons of Newport, Monmouthshire in May 1965.

The East Asiatic Company itself was founded in Copenhagen in 1897, initially to provide passenger and freight services between the Danish Capital, Bangkok and the Far East. The business grew considerably, but as air travel become more popular its passenger operations shrank, these being abandoned in 1969. From 1981 to 1992, the firm withdrew from shipping altogether. It was later rebranded as the Santa Fe Group. *Derek Penney*

**Below:** BR Bulleid Battle of Britain Class 4-6-2 No. 34072 "257 Squadron" leads "The Cunarder" westwards at Earlsfield in September 1964. Originally incorporating both Pullmans and ordinary passenger accommodation, the train, which was run in connection with sailings of Cunard Line's RMS Queen Mary and RMS Queen Elizabeth, was introduced in July 1952, with its first departure from Waterloo appropriately being worked by Bulleid Merchant Navy Class 4-6-2 No. 35004 "Cunard White Star". A similar train, named "The Statesman", provided a connection between Waterloo and Southampton Docks for those sailing on United States Lines' SS United States, with other such services including the "Union Castle Express", the "Holland American" and the "South American". *Derek Penney*

**Below:** Rebuilt Bulleid Merchant Class 4-6-2 No. 35012 "United States Line" approaches Surbiton with a Bournemouth-bound express on 23 July 1966. The second locomotive to be built under Order No. 1189, No. 35012 was outshopped from Eastleigh Works in January 1945 as No. 21C12. It entered service at Nine Elms wearing wartime black but lost this livery soon after, being repainted into malachite green ahead of its official naming, which was carried out by Admiral Schuirmann of the United States Navy in a ceremony at Waterloo station on 10 April 1945. It was the first of Merchant Navies to wear malachite green after No. 21C2 "Union Castle" was repainted into wartime black in May 1944. Its renumbering into the BR number series came in March 1949. Following further repaints, firstly into BR express blue in February 1951 and then BR green in July 1952, the locomotive was transferred to Bournemouth depot in January 1954. It was not to stay there for long, however, and was reallocated to Nine Elms in May that year. There it stayed until being transferred Weymouth in August 1964, by which point it had been rebuilt into the condition in which it is illustrated here, it emerging from Eastleigh after rebuilding in February 1957. After returning to Nine Elms once more, it was withdrawn in March 1967. It travelled a total of 1 134 836 miles during its 22 years of service. *Dave Marriot*

**Above:** Heavily weathered and shorn of its nameplates, rebuilt Bulleid Merchant Navy Class 4-6-2 No. 35024 "East Asiatic Company" speeds westwards through Esher on 23 July 1966. *Dave Marriot*

**Above right:** With its number painted on the smokebox door in place of its missing numberplate, rebuilt Bulleid Battle of Britain Class 4-6-2 No. 34088 "213 Squadron" heads a Bournemouth-bound express through Weybridge on 1 June 1966. The locomotive, which was named after a fighter squadron that was based at Exeter at the start of the Battle of Britain but later moved to RAF Tangmere in Kent, was built at Brighton Works in December 1948 and was the last of seven Light Pacifics to receive experimental apple green livery, which was carried until December 1950. It spent most of its life working on the South Eastern Division of BR's Southern Region, being based at Ramsgate until a move to Stewarts Lane in October 1954. Rebuilt at Eastleigh Works in April 1960 after accumulating 377 016 miles in its original form, the locomotive was moved to Nine Elms in May 1961. But for a short loan to Brighton from June to July 1963, it remained at Nine Elms until September 1964. At the time of this photograph, the locomotive was based at Eastleigh, from where it was withdrawn in March 1967 with a total mileage of 656 583. It was scrapped by John Cashmore Ltd of Newport, Monmouthshire in March 1968. *Dave Marriot*

**Below:** Rebuilt Bulleid Battle of Britain Class 4-6-2 No. 34077 "603 Squadron" passes Esher with a Down express on 23 July 1966. Just behind the photographer (on the opposite side of the line) there were two excursion platforms, which were once used to provide additional capacity at the station when races were held at the nearby Sandown Park racecourse. *Dave Marriot*

**Below right:** In a scene reminiscent of the days of the "Bournemouth Belle", rebuilt Bulleid Merchant Navy Class 4-6-2 No. 35028 "Clan Line" lays down a smokescreen at Weybridge on the morning of 6 November 2021 as its heads south with UK Railtours' "Hampshire Pullman" charter. As per the route indicator discs, this was to take the Portsmouth Direct Line from Woking; however, the train had originated from Victoria rather than Waterloo and was to avoid Portsmouth, it instead heading to Eastleigh to return to the Capital via the South West Main Line.

Built at Eastleigh Works as part of Order No. 3393, which represented the final batch of Merchant Navies, Nos. 35021–35030, No. 35028 entered service in December 1948. It was initially based at Bournemouth motive power depot but was moved to Dover Marine in October 1949. It remained on the former Eastern Section, being used to work boat trains and also the "Golden Arrow" and "Night Ferry" services for over a decade, although for the majority of this time (from March 1950 to May 1959) it was allocated to Stewarts Lane. It was while it was based there that the locomotive gained its name, this being officially unveiled in a ceremony at Southampton Docks on 15 January 1951 by Lord Rotherwick, the then Chairman of the shipping line. Displaced as a result of the Kent Coast electrification, its final years were spent on the Southern Region's South Western Division. Having been reallocated to Nine Elms, in October 1959 the locomotive was rebuilt at Eastleigh Works, it being the last

of the class to be so dealt with. In August 1964, it was transferred to Weymouth, remaining there until being moved back to Nine Elms in March 1967, from where it was eventually withdrawn upon the end of Southern Region steam on 9 July 1967 with a total mileage of 794 391.

The locomotive was sold straight into preservation, it being purchased by the Merchant Navy Locomotive Preservation Society, a volunteer-led charity, which was founded with the intention of saving one of the locomotives and maintaining it in working order, for the sum of £2200. "Clan Line" was chosen on account of it being the last member of the class to receive a major repair, and of the locomotives that were available at the time, its boiler was thought to be in the best condition. It was initially based at the Longmoor Military Railway in Hampshire, then at nearby Liss, and has since had several homes, it eventually returning its former base at Stewarts Lane in 1999. Apart from when it has been undergoing overhaul, the locomotive has been in continuous use on the main line since 1974 and is widely regarded as one of the most reliable locomotives in preservation. *Rhys Jones*

**Left:** With steam feathering at its safety valves, a testament to the excellent steam-raising capabilities of the Bulleid boilers, rebuilt Merchant Navy Class 4-6-2 No. 35029 "Ellerman Lines" passes West Byfleet with an express service heading towards Bournemouth in September 1964. Note how well kept the linesides are in comparison with today. As is shown by the bare earth in the background, cinders from passing steam locomotives would often set any lineside vegetation alight, leaving only scorched earth behind. *Derek Penney*

**Right:** Whistle blaring, rebuilt Bulleid Battle of Britain Class 4-6-2 No. 34077 "603 Squadron" speeds through Woking on 22 August 1966. The photographer recalls that this was taken on the first full day of travelling using an All Line rail rover ticket. He had travelled from Shrewsbury to Paddington overnight, being hauled into the former GWR terminus by a "Western" (Class 52) diesel-hydraulic locomotive, which would have been relatively new at the time. Being more interested in the outgoing steam traction, he failed to record the locomotive's number, something which he now regrets as the entirety of the class had been withdrawn within a decade or so of this.

Built at Brighton Works in July 1948, No. 34077 was based for the first 13 years of its life on the South Eastern Division of the Southern Region, it initially being allocated to Ramsgate motive power depot. Apart from a short spell at Stewarts Lane between December 1948 and November 1949, it remained at Ramsgate until December 1957. After returning to Stewarts Lane, it was then transferred to the South Western Division, being based at Nine Elms from December 1957 to August 1964. It was whilst it was allocated there that the locomotive was rebuilt into the form in which it is seen here, this taking place at Eastleigh Works in July 1960 after it had travelled a distance of 478 162 miles. The locomotive ended its days at Eastleigh shed, where it was based at the time of this photograph, it eventually being withdrawn in March 1967. It was subsequently sold to John Cashmore Ltd of Newport, Monmouthshire and was scrapped in August 1967.

With its headquarters in Edinburgh, 603 Squadron was formed as an Auxiliary Air Force Squadron in 1925 at RAF (Royal Air Force) Turnhouse. Shortly after the outbreak of World War II, the squadron brought down a Junkers Ju 88 bomber that was flying over the Firth of Forth, this being the first enemy aircraft to be shot down over the skies of the UK since 1918. Having been moved to RAF Hornchurch in Essex in 1940, the squadron became involved in the Battle of Britain, it going on to be highest scoring Battle of Britain fighter squadron. In 1942, it was redeployed to defend Malta, later being converted to a maritime strike squadron operating out of North Africa. The squadron was eventually disbanded at the end of the war but has since been reformed. *Rhys Jones*

**Left:** Ex-SR Bulleid Battle of Britain Class 4-6-2 No. 34057 "Biggin Hill" heads an Up stopping train including an interesting array of non-passenger-carrying coaching stock past West Byfleet in September 1964. One of the Light Pacifics that was loaned to the Great Eastern during the early 1950s, the locomotive was built at Brighton Works in March 1947 as part of Order No. 3213 and was numbered as No. 21C157 until June 1949. It was initially based on the Eastern Section of the SR at Stewarts Lane motive power depot but spent most of its life operating over former LSWR metals on the South Western Division of BR's Southern Region, being allocated at this point to Salisbury shed. Later becoming the last unrebuilt Battle of Britain in service with BR, it was withdrawn shortly before the end of Southern Region steam, in May 1967, and was scrapped by John Cashmore Ltd of Newport, Monmouthshire during October 1967. *Derek Penney*

**Above:** Rebuilt Bulleid Battle of Britain Class 4-6-2 No. 34109 "Sir Trafford Leigh Mallory" passes Farnborough, a favourite location of the photographer, with an Up West of England Line train on 6 September 1962. Built at Brighton Works as part of Order No. 3496, at a reported cost of £24 784, the locomotive had entered service at Bournemouth motive power depot a little over 12 years earlier, in May 1950. It was reallocated to Exmouth Junction, its home at the time of this photograph being taken, in February 1958. Having accumulated 557 217 miles, the locomotive was rebuilt at Eastleigh Works in March 1961, it being one of the last four Light Pacifics to be so treated. Upon its release from Eastleigh it would see only another three and half years of service, during which time it covered another 162 601 miles, which raises the question of whether its rebuilding was really worth it. After its withdrawal in September 1964, the locomotive lingered at Exmouth Junction until November of that year, by which point it had been sold on to Birds of Morriston, Swansea for disposal. Its scrapping eventually came in December 1966. The locomotive wore BR green livery for its entire career.

Born in July 1892, Sir Trafford Leigh-Mallory commanded No. 12 (Fighter) Group during the Battle of Britain and shortly after this took over the command of No. 11 (Fighter) Group from Sir Keith Park to defend the skies over south-east England. He has come in for much criticism over his support of the Big Wing policy, whereby a number of squadrons operated together after taking off to provide mutual protection and reduce casualties when engaged in battle with the Luftwaffe. Park said that such formations were unwieldy, difficult to manoeuvre and rarely in the right place at the right time, and because of this he believed that No. 12 Group was not doing enough to protect the airfields in the South-East. Leigh-Mallory, however, said that not enough was being done to allow the mass fighter formations to operate successfully. This opinion was shared by Charles Portal, who became the Chief of Air Staff after the Battle of Britain and duly removed Sir Keith Park from his position. Once in charge of No. 11 Group, the offensively-minded Leigh-Mallory went on to introduce wing-sized formations when undertaking raids over the skies of France, but these did not have the intended effect, with the RAF suffering heavy losses as a result. In 1942, he was appointed as Commander-in-Chief of Fighter Command, later being made Commander-in-Chief of the Allied Expeditionary Air Force ahead of the invasion of Normandy. He was killed in November 1944 when an aircraft on which he was travelling to Ceylon to take up the post of Air Commander-in-Chief South East Asia Command crashed into the French Alps in poor weather. *Dave Marriot*

**Above:** Looking in the opposite direction, BR Standard Class 4MT 4-6-0 No. 75078 is pictured approaching Farnborough on 28 September 1964. Built at Swindon Works in January 1956, this locomotive saw less than ten years' service with BR. It was allocated to the Southern Region throughout, initially to Exmouth Junction motive power depot, then to Basingstoke (from June 1956), Nine Elms (from April 1963) and latterly at Eastleigh (from June 1965). Following its withdrawal in July 1966, it was sold to Woodham Brothers Ltd of Barry. Having arrived at the South Wales scrapyard in November 1966, it was saved for preservation by the Standard Four Locomotive Society in 1972 and was moved to the Keighley & Worth Valley Railway in June that year. It was returned to steam within five years of its arrival at the West Yorkshire line and has since enjoyed several spells of operation there. *Dave Marriot*

**Below:** At the head of a Bournemouth-bound express, rebuilt Bulleid Merchant Navy Class 4-6-2 No. 35008 "Orient Line" overtakes BR Standard Class 5MT 4-6-0 No. 73082 "Camelot" on a local stopping service at Farnborough on 14 September 1963.

Constructed at Eastleigh Works as part of Order No. 1068, the Merchant Navy entered service at Salisbury in June 1942 wearing wartime black livery. It was named in a ceremony at Waterloo station on 2 November 1942 by Mr I C Geddes, who was then the Chairman of Orient Line. After being involved in a collision with an EMU while running into Waterloo on 10 June 1947, which caused considerable damage to its front end, the locomotive was given an overhaul at Eastleigh Works. Whilst there it was repainted into malachite green livery, it being the last of the locomotives to be so treated. It carried this livery for around two years before once again being repainted, this time into BR express blue, becoming No. 35008 at the same time. It carried this guise until May 1952, when it was repainted into BR green, which it wore for the remainder of its life. Having been reallocated to Bournemouth in January 1954, the locomotive was transferred to Exmouth Junction in August of that same year. It was whilst based there that it was rebuilt, this taking place at Eastleigh Works in May 1957. The locomotive returned to Bournemouth in February 1960. It remained there for around six years before being transferred to Weymouth, where it was based from October 1966 to March 1967, after which it was based at Nine Elms until its withdrawal from service upon the end of Southern Region steam in July 1967. During its 25 years of service, it travelled some 1 286 418 miles. The locomotive was disposed of by J Buttigieg of Newport, Monmouthshire in October 1968.

No. 73082, meanwhile, was built at Derby Works in July 1955. It was based on the Southern Region throughout its short life, initially working out of Stewarts Lane shed. The electrification of the Kent Coast route prompted its reallocation to Nine Elms in May 1959, where it was based at the time of this photograph being taken. The modernisation of the South Western Division and the reduced demand for steam traction that this brought about then saw the locomotive moved to the semi-roundhouse at Guildford in May 1965, from where it was eventually withdrawn in June 1966. The locomotive was subsequently sold to Woodham Brothers Ltd of Barry but was saved for preservation in 1979 by the 73082 Camelot Locomotive Society. It has since been returned to service at the Bluebell Railway in Sussex. *Dave Marriot*

**Above:** Rebuilt Bulleid West Country Class 4-6-2 No. 34045 "Ottery St. Mary" heads an Up express through Farnborough on 14 September 1963. The last locomotive to be built as part of Order No. 2885, No. 34045 was outshopped from Brighton Works in October 1946 carrying No. 21C145. It gained its BR number and its name, which comes from a town in the eastern part of Devon on the River Otter, in December 1948. A repaint into BR green livery followed in May 1950, while its rebuilding came in October 1958, by which point the locomotive had travelled 521 956 miles. As it had received an overhaul during the previous year, its rebuilding might have come as something of a surprise to enthusiasts at the time; however, it re-entered the works in July 1958 for an unscheduled overhaul and its rebuilding was carried out at the same time as this. The work took 11 weeks rather than the usual six, meaning that No. 34073 "249 Squadron", which also visited the works for an overhaul around this time, was released back into traffic in its original air-smoothed form. Having been withdrawn from service at Bournemouth in June 1964 with a total mileage of 761 465, No. 34045 was scrapped by Woodham Brothers Ltd of Barry in May 1965. It was one of only two Bulleid Pacifics to be cut up by the South Wales scrap merchant, the other being No. 34094 "Morthoe". *Dave Marriot*

**Right:** Bulleid West Country Class 4-6-2 No. 34099 "Lynmouth" passes Farnborough on 6 September 1962. Named after the picturesque coastal village in north Devon that straddles the confluence of the East and West Lyn rivers and sits in a gorge 700 ft below neighbouring Lynton, to which it is connected by a funicular railway, No. 34099 was built under BR at Eastleigh Works in December 1949 as part of Order No. 3486. It spent most of its early life on the former Eastern Section of the SR network, being based at Ramsgate motive power depot until November 1952. Following a month at Salisbury, it returned to Ramsgate and remained there until February 1958, after which it was based at

Bournemouth until February 1959. At the time of this photograph, the locomotive was shedded at Salisbury. It was withdrawn from service in November 1964 with a recorded mileage of 628 771 and was scrapped by Birds of Morriston, Swansea in March 1965. *Dave Marriot*

**Above:** Ex-SR Bulleid West Country Class 4-6-2 No. 34007 "Wadebridge" passes Farnborough on 14 September 1963 with a service from Waterloo to Southampton Terminus. Built at Brighton in August 1945 as part of Order No. 2561, the locomotive was originally referred to as No. 21C107 and was allocated from new to Exmouth Junction motive power depot, from where it worked services to Barnstaple, Ilfracombe, Plymouth, Salisbury and over the "Withered Arm" into Cornwall. It was officially named by Mr C H Paul, Chairman of the Wadebridge Rural Council, in a ceremony at the Cornish town's station on 31 October 1945. Renumbering came in March 1949 and, having been transferred to Nine Elms the previous month, in May 1951 the locomotive lost its malachite green livery in favour of a coat of BR green. It remained at Nine Elms until September 1964, after which it was based at Salisbury shed for the final year of its career, being withdrawn from service in October 1965 having travelled a total of 823 193 miles. It was subsequently sold to Woodham Brothers Ltd for scrap, arriving at Barry in May 1966, but languished there until being bought for preservation by the Plym Valley Railway in May 1981. Later sold to a small group of enthusiasts who intended to return it to traffic, the locomotive was moved to the Bodmin & Wenford Railway and after a lengthy restoration made its first moves under its own steam in over 40 years in October 2006. It is now based at the Mid Hants Railway. *Dave Marriot*

**Right:** In addition to the many services on the South Western Main Line, visiting the Farnborough area also enabled enthusiasts to observe the comings and goings on the lines between Redhill and Reading (the North Downs Line) and between Ascot and Ash Vale. With the main line running along the embankment in the background, ex-SR Maunsell N Class 2-6-0 No. 31872 heads a local service along the North Downs Line on 6 September 1962.

Originally designed for mixed-traffic work on the South Eastern & Chatham Railway (SECR), the N Classes eventually found use across most of the SR network and examples remained in service with BR until as late as 1966. No. 31872, which was one of 50 locomotives that were built by the SR at Ashford Works using parts produced at the Royal Arsenal at Woolwich, was withdrawn from service at Redhill less than a year after this photograph was taken, however, in May 1963. After almost 38 years of operation, it was scrapped at Eastleigh Works in August 1963. *Dave Marriot*

**Right:** Ex-SR Maunsell U Class 2-6-0 No. 31801 passes Farnborough with a westbound service on 6 September 1962.

Outwardly similar to Maunsell's earlier N Class but with 6 ft diameter driving wheels, the U Class was developed in the late 1920s to meet a need for a two-cylinder tender engine to work cross-country and semi-fast services. At the time these duties were undertaken by Maunsell's K Class 2-6-4Ts, which had limited water capacity and were found to be rough riding when travelling at speed over poorly maintained track, resulting in several derailments. Following an incident at Sevenoaks in August 1927 in which 13 people were killed, the entire class was withdrawn. With parts already on order for further K Class locomotives, the decision was made to use these in the construction of the new U Class 2-6-0s, while the existing tank engines were to be rebuilt, this involving the removal of the side tanks, coal bunker and trailing axle from each of the locomotives. They retained their original numbers, but their names were lost due to the bad publicity associated with these after the Sevenoaks derailment. Rebuilt locomotives could be easily identified even without referring to their numbers as they had low running plates, tall splashers, double spectacle plates in the cab front and large cabside cutaways.

One of the 20 locomotives that were built as tank engines, No. 31801 was converted into a 2-6-0 at Ashford Works in July 1928, at which point it carried No. A801 (it was previously named "River Darenth"). It was renumbered as No. 1801 in the early 1930s, becoming No. 31801 in May 1948. After almost 36 years of service as a 2-6-0, it was withdrawn from service at Guildford in June 1964 and its scrapping was undertaken by John Cashmore Ltd of Newport, Monmouthshire during December that year.
*Dave Marriot*

**Right:** With a train made up of what mostly appears to be Maunsell stock in tow, ex-SR Bulleid Battle of Britain Class 4-6-2 No. 34054 "Lord Beaverbrook" passes Cove, between Fleet and Farnborough, while heading for Waterloo. Unfortunately, the photograph is undated; however, we can narrow it down to having been taken between October 1959, when the locomotive gained late BR crests on its tender, and March 1963, when its tender raves were removed. A feature that was carried over from the earlier Merchant Navy locomotives, these served no real purpose and caused problems when it came to replenishing coal and water supplies. They also trapped water, which accelerated rates of corrosion, and limited locomotive crews' vision when running tender first. In order to overcome these problems, the raves were experimentally removed from the tenders that were paired with No. 34011 "Tavistock", No. 34059 "Sir Archibald Sinclair" and No. 34065 "Hurricane" during 1952. Although successful, there were no more cut-down tenders produced for the Light Pacifics until a programme of modifications was started in 1957. All but five of the tenders were so treated. *Derek Penney*

**Above right:** Looking much better than its rebuilt counterpart pictured below, albeit shorn of its nameplates, ex-SR Bulleid West Country Class 4-6-2 No. 34019 "Bideford" heads in the Down direction through Fleet sometime towards the end of steam on the Southern Region.

One of the earlier Light Pacifics, the locomotive, then known as No. 21C119, was built at the SR's Brighton Works in December 1945. It was officially named by the then mayor of the north Devon market town, William Chubb, in a ceremony at Bideford station on 29 August 1946. Around a year later the locomotive was converted to oil burning, it being one of only two members of the class to be so treated, the other being No. 21C136, which later became No. 34036 "Westward Ho". It had been intended that as many as 30 Light Pacifics would have been converted to oil burners; however, not long after the second locomotive was released back into traffic it was discovered that the fuel was no longer cheaply available, which led to the programme being cancelled. Both locomotives had been converted back to being coal burners by the summer of 1948, by which point No. 21C119 had become No. 34019.

The locomotive had an interesting allocation history. Based at Exmouth Junction from new, it was transferred to Eastleigh in April 1948. It returned to Exmouth Junction in September 1948, staying there until March 1951. This was followed by a move to Nine Elms, which was home to the locomotive until September 1958, when it was transferred to Brighton. After almost five years at the south coast shed, it was on the move again. From August 1963 to August 1964, it was shedded at Salisbury, then, until November 1964, at Feltham, eventually moving to Eastleigh, from where it was reallocated to Nine Elms in June 1966. Withdrawal came in March 1967, by which point the locomotive had covered a total of 701 316 miles; it was duly sold to John Cashmore Ltd of Newport, Monmouthshire for scrapping. Within six months of it being taken out of service, the locomotive was no more.

Just to the left of the locomotive, behind the Up platform, is Fleet Pond, the largest freshwater lake in Hampshire, after which the station was originally named. The construction of the railway bisected the pond, which was at one time used by the War Department (WD) as training ground. Indeed, in 1897, the LSWR had to purchase land from the WD in order for the line to be widened and a new station and goods yard to be constructed. In the years that followed, the company applied to build a new workshop in the area; however, the local council refused the request so as to maintain the rural nature of the area. The works was instead built at Eastleigh. *Dave Marriot*

**Right:** In an undated scene that based upon the locomotive's unkempt condition and the presence of the newly installed 750 V DC conductor rails is presumed to be from the latter years of Southern Region steam, rebuilt Bulleid Battle of Britain Class 4-6-2 No. 34059 "Sir Archibald Sinclair" is pictured passing through Fleet heading in the direction of Waterloo.

One of only three rebuilt Battle of Britains to survive into preservation, the locomotive, which was originally known as No. 21C159, was built at Brighton Works in April 1947 and was allocated from new to Nine Elms motive power depot. But for brief periods on loan to the Great Eastern Division of the Eastern Region in 1949 and the early 1950s and later to the South Eastern Division of the Southern Region in the early 1960s, it spent almost all its life working services to and from the South-West of England, being transferred from Nine Elms to Exmouth Junction in March 1951 and then to Salisbury in October 1955. It was whilst it was shedded at Salisbury that the locomotive was rebuilt, this taking place at Eastleigh Works towards the start of 1960. The locomotive remained in service until May 1966, by which point it had covered some 877 107 miles, 569 583 of which were whilst it was in its original form. Following its withdrawal by BR, the locomotive was sold to Woodham Brothers Ltd of Barry, arriving at the South Wales scrapyard in October 1966. Like many of the other locomotives there, its tender was sold to one of the local steelworks for use as an ingot carrier, while the locomotive itself was eventually sold to a preservation group based at the Bluebell Railway in Sussex. After a lengthy restoration, which included the construction of new tender, it was returned to steam in 2008.

Named after the one-time leader of the Liberal Party who held the position of Secretary of State for Air under Churchill's coalition government from 1940 to May 1945 and was the Honorary Air Commodore of 600 (City of London) Squadron, Royal Auxiliary Air Force from 1941 to 1949, the locomotive holds the distinction of being the first to be named following the formation of BR, its naming being undertaken by Sir Archibald Sinclair himself in a ceremony at Waterloo station on 24 February 1948. Whilst there, the former Air Minister also christened No. 21C157 "Biggin Hill", which was one of the fighter stations at the forefront of the Battle of Britain and at that point the base of 600 Squadron. *Dave Marriot*

**Below:** Ex-SR Bulleid Battle of Britain Class 4-6-2 No. 34064 "Fighter Command" passes Potbridge, near Winchfield, with a boat train bound for Southampton Docks in the September of 1965.

The 1000th locomotive to be built at Brighton Works, No. 34064 entered traffic as No. 21C164 in July 1947, initially allocated to Ramsgate motive power depot. Its naming was carried out by Vice Chief of the Air Staff Sir James Robb at Waterloo station on 11 September 1947 in a joint ceremony with the namings of No. 21C151 "Winston Churchill" and No. 21C152 "Lord Dowding". Having been transferred to Nine Elms, the locomotive lost its original malachite green livery in favour of an experimental apple green in June 1948, it also being renumbered as No. 34064 around this time. In December 1948, it was then moved to Stewarts Lane, but returned to Nine Elms in March 1950 before being repainted into BR green in June that year. The locomotive remained at Nine Elms until May 1959, it then being reallocated to Exmouth Junction, where it was based for three years. After another spell at Nine Elms, from May 1962 to December 1963, it was transferred to Eastleigh. Whilst there, in 1965 it was placed on standby to work Sir Winston Churchill's funeral train but was not needed. Following a transfer to Salisbury in October 1965, the locomotive was withdrawn from service in May 1966 after it suffered a high-speed slip somewhere between Farnborough and Basingstoke that resulted in its coupling rods being bent. It covered a total of 759 666 miles during its 19 years of operation. The locomotive was scrapped by the Bird Group at Bridgend in November 1966.

It is not immediately obvious from the angle at which this photograph was taken, but the locomotive was at this point fitted with a Giesl oblong ejector instead of the usual Lemaître blast pipe, which it replaced in April 1962. The invention of Austrian Dr Adolph Giesl-Gieslingen, the ejector, consisting of multiple fan-shaped nozzles in a line exhausting into a narrow chimney, was primarily intended to improve the performance of steam locomotives by increasing blast pipe suction draught to make better use of energy, which helped to both reduce coal consumption and increase power output, enabling faster acceleration. This meant that schedules could either be sped up or heavier loads could be hauled without having an adverse impact upon timings. The greater velocity at which exhaust left the ejector, combined with the narrow frontal area and greater height of the chimney, also helped with smoke lifting. The main reason for No. 34064 being fitted with a Giesl ejector was, however, to prevent the emission of sparks. Prior to this, numerous experiments had been carried out on the Light Pacifics to try and solve the problem, but the installation of spark arresting equipment ruined their free-steaming capabilities, the original exhaust arrangement being unable to produce enough draught to overcome the extra resistance to the gas flow that the spark arrestor plates or mesh caused. The greater efficiency of the Giesl ejector was expected to resolve this. Indeed, it was found to be very successful and thereafter the locomotive was well regarded by footplate crews. It wasn't without its problems, though. When it was first fitted to the locomotive, it increased the draw on the fire to such an extent that the brick arch and superheater ends were burnt away, while the steel rim protecting the fire hole melted. Apart from No. 34092 "City of Wells", which gained a Giesl ejector in preservation, No. 34064 was the only member of the class to be modified in this way. Considering how it improved the locomotive's performance, this may sound surprising; however, the licence fee that had to be paid apparently put BR off. *Derek Penney*

**Above:** With a variety of different designs of coaching stock, including several Staniers, a solitary Thompson and a number of the ubiquitous BR Mark 1s, in tow, ex-SR Bulleid West Country Class 4-6-2 No. 34015 "Exmouth" passes Potbridge with a Down West of England train in September 1965. Built at Brighton Works as part of Order No. 2561 in November 1945, the locomotive was allocated from new to Exmouth Junction motive power depot, where it spent much of its later life. Originally known as No. 21C115 and painted in malachite green livery, it was officially named by Exmouth's Mayor, Councillor J Down, in a ceremony at the town's station on 26 June 1946. No. 21C114 was officially named "Budleigh Salterton" on the same date, while a series of local naming ceremonies saw Nos. 21C120, 21C118 and 21C110 respectively named "Seaton", "Axminster" and "Sidmouth" during that week. After being repainted into BR green in January 1950, the locomotive was briefly transferred to Salisbury shed, it being based there between January 1951 and March 1951. After a further 13 years and five months at Exmouth Junction, it returned to Salisbury in August 1964 and was withdrawn from there in April 1967. The locomotive was scrapped by John Cashmore Ltd of Newport, Monmouthshire during September 1967.
*Dave Marriot*

**Right:** Viewed from the opposite side of the line, rebuilt Bulleid Merchant Navy Class 4-6-2 No. 35028 "Clan Line" heads south with 1Z82 10.43 Victoria–Haslemere, the outbound leg of UK Railtours' "King Alfred" charter, at Potbridge on 10 February 2018. But for the modernisation of the railway infrastructure, the scene has changed surprisingly little over the intervening 50 years.
*Rhys Jones*

**Left:** BR Standard Class 5MT 4-6-0 No. 73118 heads west at Hook on 7 June 1965.

Largely based on Stanier's "Black 5" 4-6-0s, 842 of which were built between 1934 and 1951 – these being, arguably, the most successful mixed-traffic locomotives in Britain at the time, the Standard 5MTs were intended to build on their predecessor's success by making maintenance and operation cheaper and easier. This they did by incorporating components that were shared with the other BR Standard classes, plus innovations such as self-cleaning smokeboxes and rocking grates, which made it quicker and easier for their crews to dispose of the engines at the end of their duties. 172 of the locomotives were built between April 1951 and June 1957, 20 of which were allocated new to the Southern Region. Nos. 73080–73089 went to Stewarts Lane to work services to the Kent coast, while Nos. 73110–73119 were allocated to Nine Elms. The latter locomotives were notable in that they were paired with BR1F tenders, which had a water capacity of 5625 gallons, the greatest of all the tender types used with the locomotives (although Nos. 73080–73089 faced a similar lack of water troughs on the South Eastern Division, they were given BR1B tenders). The electrification of the Chatham Main Line in the late 1950s saw the Standard 5s that were based at Stewarts Lane later transferred to the South Western Division of the Southern Region.

Built at Doncaster Works in December 1956, No. 73118 was based at Nine Elms until August 1964. During this time, it carried the name "King Leodegrance", which had previously been carried by ex-LSWR Urie N15 Class 4-6-0 No. 30739, which was withdrawn in May 1957. By the time that this photograph was taken, however, the plates had been removed from the locomotive, which was then an Eastleigh engine. It was based there until June 1966, after which it was returned to Nine Elms for a short period before being reallocated to the semi-roundhouse at Guildford in September 1966. The locomotive remained there until the end of steam on the Southern Region in July 1967. After being in operation for only a little over ten years, it was sold to John Cashmore Ltd of Newport, Monmouthshire for scrap and was dismantled during April 1968. *Dave Marriot*

**Above:** Rebuilt Bulleid Merchant Navy Class No. 35024 "East Asiatic Company" is pictured working the Down "Bournemouth Belle" at Basingstoke on 16 May 1964. The prestigious Pullman train was introduced by the SR in 1931 to provide a means by which the more well-off could travel to and from the increasingly popular resort but was withdrawn upon the end of Southern Region steam in July 1967. *Dave Marriot*

**Left:** No. 35005 "Canadian Pacific", one of the first batch of Bulleid's Merchant Navy Class Pacifics, powers past Hook on 7 June 1965. The locomotive was withdrawn from service just a matter of months later, in October 1965, by which point it had covered a total of 976 806 miles. It was the only one of the first 14 members of the class not to exceed one million miles during its working life. This, it is believed, was because the locomotive was trialled with a Berkeley mechanical stoker between March 1948 and April 1951, which limited its availability. Acquired second-hand from Canada, the stoker was intended to enable to the locomotive to operate more efficiently than when it was fired manually by increasing the rate at which coal was delivered to the firebox but was ultimately unsuccessful. Large lumps of coal caused the equipment to become blocked; the fire was difficult to control, which meant that steaming was erratic; and the locomotive's already high coal consumption was increased by around 25%, primarily as a result of an increase in unburnt fuel loss. Not only this, there was, in fact, a small reduction in efficiency, as steam was needed to drive the stoker. It was therefore concluded that the investment could only be justified where the amount of coal needed to fire a locomotive in normal service exceeded the capability of a single fireman. *Dave Marriot*

**Above:** Rebuilt Bulleid West Country Class 4-6-2 No. 34031 "Torrington" heads an express made up mostly of Bulleid coaching stock through the cutting just outside of Basingstoke station on 16 May 1964. Introduced into service as No. 21C131 in June 1946, the locomotive was constructed at Brighton Works as part of Order No. 2885. For the first few years of its life it was an Eastern Section engine, but in November 1949, by which point it had become No. 34031, it was transferred from Stewarts Lane to Exmouth Junction. It was around the time of this move that the locomotive was repainted into BR green livery and gained its name, the unveiling of which was carried out by Alderman E A Holwill, Mayor of Torrington, in a ceremony at the north Devon town's station. But for a brief loan to Nine Elms between November 1950 and April 1951, it remained at Exmouth Junction until February 1959. Having been rebuilt at Eastleigh Works in December 1958, it then returned to Nine Elms for a lengthier stay, being based there until August 1964, after which it was sent to Eastleigh. The locomotive was withdrawn at Eastleigh in February 1965 and was sold to John Cashmore Ltd of Newport, Monmouthshire soon afterwards, it being scrapped in May 1965. *Dave Marriot*

**Right:** A rare capture of a Bulleid Battle of Britain Class 4-6-2 working a mineral train. No. 34068 "Kenley" heads in the Up direction along the Slow Line away from Basingstoke on 1 September 1961. Having been built at Brighton Works, the locomotive entered traffic with the SR in October 1947 as No. 21C168. It was named in February of the following year after one of the RAF's three main fighter stations responsible for defending the skies of London (the others being Biggin Hill and Croydon) and was renumbered as No. 34068 that November. Reallocated from Ramsgate to Stewarts Lane in November 1949, the locomotive lost its malachite green in September 1950. Other than receiving a cut-down tender and other relatively minor modifications, its appearance then remained largely unchanged until the end of its career, the locomotive being withdrawn from Salisbury, where it had been based since May 1961, in December 1963 with a total mileage of 700 417. It was scrapped at Eastleigh Works in March 1964. *Dave Marriot*

**Above:** Rebuilt Bulleid Merchant Navy Class 4-6-2 No. 35006 "Peninsular & Oriental S. N. Co." approaches Basingstoke with a Down West of England train on 1 August 1964. Despite its external appearance, the locomotive was withdrawn within a matter of weeks of this photograph being taken. Built at Eastleigh Works in December 1941 as part of Order No. 1068, it had entered traffic as No. 21C6 wearing malachite green livery in January 1942. Ahead of its naming, which was carried out at Ashford Works on 4 June 1942 by Sir W Currie, Chairman of P&O, it was repainted into wartime black. It remained in this guise until September 1946, when it was returned to malachite green. Having been renumbered as No. 35006 in December 1948, the locomotive carried BR express blue from March 1951 to September 1953, after which it wore BR green for the remainder of its life. Its rebuilding came in October 1959 after it had run 962 757 miles. The locomotive was withdrawn from service at Salisbury shed having covered a total of 1 134 319 miles. It was the only member of the class to remain at one shed throughout its career. It was also the only one of the 30 locomotives to have kept its original tender. Following its withdrawal, the locomotive was sold to Woodham Brothers Ltd of Barry for disposal; however, it was purchased for preservation in 1982 and moved to the embryonic Gloucestershire & Warwickshire Railway in 1983, eventually being returned to steam in 2015. *Dave Marriot*

**Above:** Heading in the Down direction, rebuilt Bulleid Battle of Britain Class 4-6-2 No. 34085 "501 Squadron" approaches Basingstoke on 1 August 1964. The discs on the front of the locomotive indicate that the train is bound for Bournemouth, its hometown at the time of this photograph being taken.

Built at Brighton Works in November 1948, the locomotive was originally used on the former Eastern Section of the SR network, being based from new at Stewarts Lane motive power depot in south London. Having had its malachite green livery replaced with BR green in March 1950, it was moved to Ramsgate in April 1951, then to Dover Marine in February 1958, eventually returning to Stewarts Lane in March 1958. Following its rebuilding at Eastleigh Works in June 1960, prior to which the locomotive had travelled 441 609 miles, it was then transferred to Bournemouth, where it remained until its withdrawal in September 1965. Having covered a total of 661 415 miles during is career, the locomotive was scrapped by J Buttigieg of Newport, Monmouthshire in April 1966.

One of 27 squadrons to have a Light Pacific named after them, 501 Squadron was based at RAF Filton, near Bristol, when the Second World War started in September 1939. In response to the attack on France, it became part of the Advanced Air Striking Force and was moved across the English Channel, being stationed at various airfields, including Anglure, Bétheniville, Dinard and Le Mans. After returning to England via St Helier, Jersey, the squadron was based at RAF Croydon, then RAF Middle Wallop in Hampshire and later RAF Gravesend in Kent, after which it served at RAF Kenley in south London. During the Battle of Britain, the squadron suffered heavy losses; more of its pilots were killed than in any other squadron. Those who survived were transferred in October 1942 to Northern Ireland, but within six months of this the squadron was returned to England, it then being based at RAF Tangmere in Kent for bomber escort work. It later went on to form part of the Air Defence of Great Britain and flew out of RAF Friston in East Sussex during Operation Overlord (the allied invasion of Normandy). After a move to RAF Manston in Kent, from where the squadron took part in an operation to intercept V-1 rockets, it was eventually disbanded at RAF Hunsdon in Hertfordshire at the end of the war in April 1945. During the conflict, its pilots were involved in over 11 000 operational sorties and shot down around 200 enemy aircraft and at least 84 rockets. *Dave Marriot*

**Right:** Heavily weathered BR Standard Class 5MT 4-6-0 No. 73171 heads in the Up direction away from Basingstoke on 12 September 1964. Numerically the last of the 172 Standard 5s, No. 73171 was outshopped from Doncaster Works in May 1957. It was initially based on the North Eastern Region at York motive power depot, moving from there to Leeds' Holbeck depot in September 1957 and then to Royston in September 1962. It was transferred to the Southern Region the following year, being based at Feltham from August 1963 to November 1964 and then at Eastleigh until its withdrawal in October 1966. *Dave Marriot*

**Above:** No. 73087 "Linette", another one of the 20 BR Standard Class 5MT 4-6-0s that were allocated new to the Southern Region in the 1950s and took the name of an ex-LSWR Urie N15 Class 4-6-0, leads a service from Southampton Terminus to Waterloo away from Basingstoke on 5 May 1964. Eagle-eyed readers will note that the locomotive has a different type of tender to its classmate that was illustrated earlier, this being paired with a smaller BR1B tender, which had a water capacity of 4725 gallons. Despite being built less than ten years earlier, it being outshopped from Doncaster Works in August 1955, the locomotive would remain in operation for only a little over two years after this photograph was taken, its withdrawal coming in October 1966. But for several spells during which it was based on the Western Region at Bath Green Park, the locomotive spent almost its entire career on the Southern Region. It was eventually scrapped by John Cashmore Ltd at Newport, Monmouthshire in April 1967. The locomotive's name comes from a woman who according to Arthurian legend travelled to King Arthur's court seeking help for her sister, Lyonesse, whose lands were under siege. *Dave Marriot*

**Right:** Collett 6100 Class "Large Prairie" 2-6-2T No. 6138 accelerates a local train away from Basingstoke towards Reading on 17 April 1960. Despite its unkempt condition, the locomotive, which was built at the GWR's Swindon Works in November 1932, would remain in service until July 1963. *Dave Marriot*

**Above:** Rebuilt Bulleid West Country Class 4-6-2 No. 34036 "Westward Ho" arrives at Basingstoke on 5 May 1964 with a train for Southampton Terminus. Another product of Brighton Works, being built as part of Order No. 2885, No. 34036 entered service in July 1946 as No. 21C136. It lost its original number in May 1948, whilst its malachite green livery was replaced by BR green in February 1952. In August 1960, after covering 582 544 miles during its first 14 years of service, the locomotive was rebuilt at Eastleigh Works. It was withdrawn with a total mileage of 894 546 at the end of Southern steam in July 1967. The locomotive was at that point based at Nine Elms, but had previously had spells at Stewarts Lane, Eastleigh, Plymouth Friary, Exmouth Junction and Salisbury sheds. It was scrapped by John Cashmore Ltd at Newport, Monmouthshire in February 1968. *Dave Marriot*

**Right:** With the main line towards Waterloo in the foreground, ex-GWR Collett 4900 Class 4-6-0 No. 4974 "Talgarth Hall" arrives at Basingstoke on 17 April 1960. Allocated at this point to Stourbridge Junction, the locomotive was outshopped from Swindon Works in January 1930 and had a service life of 32 years, it eventually being withdrawn from traffic at Gloucester in April 1962. It was scrapped at Swindon during December 1962. *Dave Marriot*

**Above:** Rebuilt Bulleid Merchant Navy Class 4-6-2 No. 35014 "Nederland Line" takes the Reading line away from Basingstoke with "The Pines Express" on 12 September 1964.

Connecting Manchester with Bournemouth, "The Pines Express" was originally routed via the former Somerset & Dorset Joint Railway (S&DJR) but was diverted via Oxford, Reading, Basingstoke and Southampton from September 1962. While it was not unusual for the Light Pacifics to appear on inter-regional workings to and from Oxford, the use of a Merchant Navy on such a service was quite a rare occurrence and it seems that as well as Dave a good number of other photographers went out to capture the event. The former GWR goods shed, a reminder that the company once had its own facilities in the town, can be seen to the right of the locomotive.

Built at Eastleigh Works as part of Order No. 1189, No. 35014 entered traffic as No. 21C14 in February 1945 wearing wartime black. It was initially allocated to Nine Elms motive power depot. Having been repainted into malachite green, it was named at Waterloo station on 27 November 1947 by Mr A F Bronsing, who was then the Managing Director of Nederland Line, in a joint ceremony with No. 21C15 "Rotterdam Lloyd". The locomotive was renumbered as No. 35014 in May 1949, repainted into BR green in August 1951 and, following transfers to Exmouth Junction (May 1954), Bournemouth (August 1954), Stewarts Lane (June 1955) and Nine Elms (June 1956), rebuilt in July 1956, by which point it had covered 516 811 miles. It was eventually withdrawn from service at Weymouth, where it had been based since September 1964, in March 1967 having accumulated a total mileage of 1 062 094 and was scrapped by John Cashmore Ltd at Newport, Monmouthshire in September that year.

The shipping line after which the locomotive was named was founded in Amsterdam in 1870 to facilitate trade between northwest Europe and the Dutch East Indies, now known as Indonesia, via the newly opened Suez Canal. The company continued to operate for almost a century, it being merged with Rotterdam Lloyd, Royal InterOcean Lines and United Netherlands Navigation Co in June 1970 to form Nedlloyd, which in 1996 merged its container shipping interests with P&O to become P&O Nedlloyd, which was in turn taken over by Maersk in 2005. *Dave Marriot*

**Right:** Although their steel fireboxes were prone to corrosion, the Bulleid Pacifics were regarded as being free steamers. Rebuilt West Country Class 4-6-2 No. 34034 "Honiton" blows off at Basingstoke while working the northbound "Pines Express" on 16 May 1964. Originally known as No. 21C134, the locomotive was built by Brighton Works in July 1946 and received its name two years later, becoming No. 34034 at around the same time. It was not until May 1950 that the locomotive lost its malachite green livery in favour of BR green, however. By this point it was based at Salisbury. Under BR ownership, it had previously had spells at Stewarts Lane (until July 1948) and Brighton (until October 1948). It remained based at Salisbury until October 1950, after which it made a brief return to Stewarts Lane (until September 1950) prior to moving to Exmouth Junction. Its stay there was just as short; in November 1950 the locomotive was moved once again, this time to Plymouth Friary, where it remained until March 1952. From there it was sent back to Exmouth Junction, this time staying there much longer. Following its rebuilding at Eastleigh Works in August 1960, the locomotive was transferred from Exmouth Junction to Eastleigh in October 1961, staying there for almost five years. It was withdrawn from service at Nine Elms, where it had been based since June 1966, upon the end of Southern Region steam in 1967 after travelling a total of 942 133 miles and was scrapped by J Buttigieg of Newport, Monmouthshire in April 1968. *Dave Marriot*

**Above:** Ex-SR Bulleid Battle of Britain Class 4-6-2 No. 34051 "Sir Winston Churchill" departs Basingstoke with an Up West of England train on 9 September 1962. One of nine Battle of Britains to survive in preservation, the locomotive had a working life of less than 20 years. It was built by the SR's Brighton Works as part of Order No. 3212 in December 1946 and entered service as No. 21C151 at Salisbury wearing malachite green. Along with No. 21C152, it was officially named by Lord Dowding in a ceremony at Waterloo station on 11 September 1947. Renumbering came in October 1948 and, following a move to Nine Elms in January 1950, the locomotive was given a coat of BR green in December of that year. In March 1951, it was transferred to Exmouth Junction, but only stayed there for several months, returning to Salisbury in June 1951. It would remain allocated to Salisbury until its withdrawal in September 1965, by which point the locomotive had covered some 807,496 miles. It is now part of the National Collection. *Dave Marriot*

**Right:** Moving to the opposite end of the station now, ex-SR Bulleid Battle of Britain Class No. 34054 "Lord Beaverbrook", one of the 50 Light Pacifics that retained their air-smoothed casing until withdrawal, gets a West of England Line train away from Basingstoke on 17 April 1960. The small clouds of steam visible in front of the first and third coupled wheelsets indicate that the sanders are being used to improve adhesion, no doubt in an effort to avoid the locomotive slipping, as they often did when working heavy trains.

Ordered as part of Order No. 3213, the locomotive was outshopped from Brighton Works in January 1947. Originally known as No. 21C154, it was officially named in a ceremony at Waterloo station on 16 September 1947, it being one of three locomotives to be named at this event. Renumbering came in March 1949, with a repaint into BR green following in April 1951. At the time of this photograph being taken, the locomotive was allocated to Salisbury shed, which had been its home since May 1952. It would remain there until October 1953, after which it was based at Exmouth Junction until being withdrawn from service in September 1964. It travelled some 737 443 miles during its 17½ years of service. Its scrapping was undertaken by the Bird Group at Bynea in March 1965.

One of 29 personalities to have a Battle of Britain locomotive named after them, Lord Beaverbrook (William Maxwell Aitken, 1st Baron of Beaverbrook) was a Canadian-born newspaper publisher who became an influential figure in British politics and the media during the first half of the 20th century. Winston Churchill, a long-standing friend of Beaverbrook's, appointed him as Minister of Aircraft Production in May 1940. In this role he overhauled aircraft production, seizing materials destined for use elsewhere and replacing the management of poor performing plants to meet increased production targets. The output of aircraft from the factories increased so much so that Churchill said it was Beaverbrook's finest hour, while Air Chief Marshal Lord Dowding, Head of Fighter Command during the Battle of Britain, said that no other man in Britain could have achieved what Beaverbrook did in maintaining the necessary supply of machines to withstand the drain of continuous battle. Beaverbrook resigned from the position in April 1941 to become Minister of State, but was later appointed as Minister of Supply, then Minister of War Production and, lastly, Lord Privy Seal, a position that he held until the end of the conflict. *Dave Marriot*

**Below:** "The Pines Express" is pictured once again, this time heading towards Bournemouth West behind Bulleid West Country Class 4-6-2 No. 34102 "Lapford" on 19 October 1963. One of the youngest of the Light Pacifics, No. 34102 was not released from Eastleigh Works until March 1950. It was allocated from new to Stewarts Lane motive power depot and remained there until February 1958, when it was transferred to Bournemouth. As can be seen from the 71B shed plate that the locomotive is carrying, it was still based at Bournemouth at the time of this photograph being taken. In fact, it remained there until August 1964. Its latter days were spent at Eastleigh, from where it was withdrawn in July 1967 having run 593 438 miles. It was disposed of by J Buttigieg of Newport, Monmouthshire the following year. *Dave Marriot*

**Above:** With a Down West of England train in tow, BR Standard Class 5MT 4-6-0 No. 73085 is pictured at Basingstoke on 22 August 1966. Built at Derby Works in August 1955, the locomotive was at first allocated to Stewarts Lane motive power depot but was loaned to Oxford from February to March 1956. After returning to Stewarts Lane, it remained there until May 1959, after which it was allocated to Nine Elms for six years or so. In October 1965, it was reallocated to Feltham, but did not stay there for long. November 1965 saw it transferred to Eastleigh, where it remained until June 1966. It was eventually withdrawn from Nine Elms in July 1967 and was scrapped by John Cashmore Ltd at Newport, Monmouthshire in April 1968. The locomotive was for a time named "Melisande", a name previously carried by ex-SR Urie N15 Class 4-6-0 No. 30753. *Rhys Jones*

**Below:** A heavily weathered rebuilt Bulleid West Country Class 4-6-2, No. 34009 "Lyme Regis", rolls into Basingstoke with an Up express on 22 August 1966. One of the 30 locomotives that were built at Brighton Works as part of Order No. 2561, No. 34009 was outshopped in September 1945 and entered service at Exmouth Junction motive power depot soon afterwards, running as No. 21C109. Its official naming was carried out by Mr H Cawley, Chairman of Axminster Urban District Council, at Axminster station on 27 August 1946. The locomotive was one of two that were named there, the other being No. 21C118 "Wincanton", which was also named by Mr H Cawley (on 25 June 1946). Having been renumbered as No. 34009 in March 1949, the locomotive lost its original malachite green livery in the December of the following year and shortly after this, in March 1951, it was reallocated to Nine Elms motive power depot in south London. Its rebuilding came in January 1961, by which point the locomotive had covered some 662 481 miles. In August 1964, it was transferred to Eastleigh, remaining there until being returned to Nine Elms in June 1966. Withdrawn with a total mileage of 959 762 in October 1966, it was later sold to J Buttigieg of Newport, Monmouthshire and was scrapped in September 1967. *Rhys Jones*

**Left:** Rebuilt Bulleid West Country Class 4-6-2 No. 34095 "Brentor" blows off steam at Basingstoke on 22 August 1966 as its tender is replenished with water ready for the journey ahead. Although water columns continued to be used for a short while after the end of steam, to replenish the steam generators that enabled diesel locomotives to provide steam heating – until this was phased out in favour of electric train heating, the majority have long since disappeared as the railway network has been modernised.

Named after a small village on the western edge of Dartmoor, No. 34095 was built as part of Order No. 3486 at Eastleigh Works in October 1949. It was introduced into service soon afterwards at Bournemouth, being based there until January 1956. It was then transferred to Nine Elms, which was its home until August 1964, by which time the locomotive had lost its air-smoothed casing and chain-driven valve gear (its rebuilding took place at Eastleigh Works in January 1961). The final three years of the locomotive's working life were spent operating out of Eastleigh, from where it was withdrawn in July 1967. It travelled a total 796 614 miles during its almost 18 year career. Its scrapping was carried out by John Cashmore Ltd at Newport, Monmouthshire in April 1968. *Rhys Jones*

**Above:** A pleasant change for the photographer from the procession of Bulleid Pacifics, ex-SR Maunsell V Class 4-4-0 No. 30918 "Hurstpierpoint" is pictured on a West of England train at Basingstoke on 8 August 1961. Despite their size, the V Class locomotives, or "Schools" as they were more commonly known, were surprisingly powerful. Intended to fulfil the requirement for an express passenger locomotive of intermediate power that could operate over main lines across the length and breadth of the SR network, including those that had short turntables, they were, in fact, the most powerful 4-4-0s (in terms of tractive effort) produced anywhere in Europe and, arguably, Richard Maunsell's most successful design.

Named after a public school in West Sussex that was founded in 1849 by Canon Nathaniel Woodard, this particular locomotive was built as part of the second batch of V Classes and was outshopped from Eastleigh Works in June 1933. It entered service as No. 918 at St Leonards shed, from where it was used to operate services over the former South Eastern Railway route between Hastings and Tonbridge. There is some disagreement as to whether the restricted loading gauge of this route influenced Maunsell's decision to use a round-topped firebox on the locomotives rather than a Belpaire firebox or whether this was a happy coincidence, but either way the locomotives were well suited to the line and crews considered them to be free steaming even when fed poor coal. The locomotive remained an Eastern Section engine for much of its life, later being based at Bricklayers Arms, Dover and Ramsgate sheds, but in May 1959 it was transferred to Nine Elms to work services over the South Western Main Line. Apart from a transfer to Brighton between April and October 1960, it was to stay at Nine Elms until the end of its career, which came in October 1961, with its scrapping being undertaken at Eastleigh Works in December 1961. *Dave Marriot*

**Above:** A couple of young enthusiasts look on as rebuilt Bulleid Merchant Navy Class 4-6-2 No. 35014 "Nederland Line" leads the Down "Atlantic Coast Express" under the signal gantry at the west end of Basingstoke station on 5 September 1962. *Dave Marriot*

**Above:** Seen from a similar position, but with the former motive power depot clearly visible in the background, BR Standard Class 5MT 4-6-0 No. 73119 "Elaine" departs Basingstoke with a Down West of England service on 1 August 1964. Its 70A shed plate indicates that the locomotive, which was built at Doncaster Works in December 1956, was at this point allocated to Nine Elms motive power depot. September 1964 would see it transferred to Eastleigh, from where it was withdrawn in March 1967. The locomotive was scrapped later that same year by John Cashmore Ltd of Newport, Monmouthshire. *Dave Marriot*

**Above:** Maunsell N15 Class 4-6-0 No. 30796 "Sir Dodinas le Savage" heads a train of Bulleid stock away from Basingstoke on 1 September 1961.

According to the number on the end of the leading carriage, No. 792, the first three vehicles are one of the three-coach L sets that were introduced on the Waterloo–West of England and Waterloo–Weymouth services in the late 1940s. Each of these consisted of two Semi-open Brake Thirds and a Corridor Composite coach, in this case Nos. 4345, 4346 and 5773. The set was withdrawn in the summer of 1967, by which point BR had abolished Third Class accommodation in favour of Second Class.

Named after a knight who fought alongside King Arthur in the Saxon Wars, the locomotive, meanwhile, was introduced into service in May 1926 and had an active life of almost 36 years, it being withdrawn from traffic at Salisbury shed in March 1962. *Dave Marriot*

**Below:** A busy scene at Basingstoke shed, with ex-SR Maunsell N15 Class 4-6-0s Nos. 30804 "Sir Cador of Cornwall" and 30765 "Sir Gareth" stabled in between duties on 6 August 1961. Note that No. 30804 has a six-wheeled tender, which it acquired from an N Class so that it could fit onto the short turntables found on the former Central Section of the SR, whereas No. 30765 has a high-capacity double-bogie tender, which was better suited to the longer routes of the former Western Section. Opened by the LSWR as a replacement for a smaller shed on the south side of the line, which was closed in 1909, this was until November 1950 one of two sheds in the town, the other being a former GWR facility located at the opposite end of the station, on the north side of the line. From then on, the Western Region locomotives that used it were serviced at the ex-LSWR shed, which was eventually closed in March 1963, although remained in use as a servicing facility until the end of Southern steam in July 1967. *Dave Marriot*

**Below:** Shortly before its transfer from Guildford to Nine Elms, Billington E4 Class 0-6-2T No. 32506 is pictured at Basingstoke shed on 17 April 1960. As this goes to show, although the 75 locomotives that made up the class were originally designed for the London, Brighton & South Coast Railway (LBSCR), their sphere of operation was broadened in their later lives, with this particular example having spells at Salisbury (from June 1951 to August 1955) and later at Eastleigh (from January 1961 until its withdrawal in June that year). *Dave Marriot*

**Above right:** 700 Class 0-6-0 No. 30368 is seen stabled at Basingstoke shed in the company of No. D 6521, a Birmingham Railway Carriage & Wagon Company Type 3 (Class 33) diesel locomotive, on 4 September 1962. Designed by Dugald Drummond and built for the LSWR by Dübs & Co of Glasgow in 1897, the 30 "Black Motors" as they became known, were good performers. Although they had some mechanical problems early in their careers, they soon settled down and were used to haul both heavy goods and secondary passenger trains across the LSWR system. To improve performance, in 1919 one of the locomotives was experimentally equipped by Urie with a superheated boiler. This required the extension of its smokebox and frames, the pitch of its boiler to be raised and some modifications to its cab. Evidently it was a success, as the other locomotives were similarly altered after the Grouping in 1923 and all but one member of the class remained in operation beyond their 60th year of service. In the case of No. 30368, which was based at Basingstoke for the entirety of its BR career, this saw 62 years' service. Having been stored in the goods yard at Basingstoke, the locomotive was moved to Eastleigh Works on 18 May 1963 and was cut up there later that year. *Dave Marriot*

**Right:** In another shed scene, ex-SR Maunsell N15 Class 4-6-0 No. 30777 "Sir Lamiel" is pictured being turned at Basingstoke on 31 July 1960.

Similar in appearance to the earlier Urie locomotives from which their design was developed, the Maunsell N15s were the first express passenger locomotives to be introduced into service by the newly formed SR in the 1920s. No. 30777 was built as part of the second batch of the locomotives, the construction of which was undertaken by the North British Locomotive Company in Glasgow (as there wasn't sufficient capacity at Eastleigh Works at the time of the order being placed). These differed from the first ten locomotives in having cabs similar to those on the Maunsell N Class 2-6-0s, which allowed the locomotives to also operate over routes on the SR's Eastern Section that had a limited loading gauge. They also had a different type of smokebox door, with clamps around the circumference rather than central tightening handles, and were paired with double-bogied tenders instead of Drummond watercarts. A third batch of the locomotives brought further differences in design, with these locomotives featuring smaller firebox grates and improved water heating surfaces. As illustrated earlier, these also had smaller six-wheeled tenders.

Around the time that the first of the locomotives were introduced into service, it was decided by the SR's newly appointed public relations officer that they should be given names connected King Arthur and the Knights of the Round Table, hence the locomotives being referred to as "King Arthurs". According to legend, Sir Lamiel was a Welsh knight who was said to be a great lover.

Within a little over a year of this photograph being taken, the locomotive was withdrawn from service. Happily, however, it survived as part of the National Collection, it being selected as replacement for the class doyen No. 30453 "King Arthur", which could not be restored to its as-built condition as there was no suitable tender available. *Dave Marriot*

**Above:** Also present on shed on 1 April 1956 was Drummond T9 Class 4-4-0 No. 30724. Known as "Greyhounds" because of the high speeds that they were capable of, the T9s were introduced by the LSWR around the turn of the 20th century to work express passenger services to the South-West of England. The majority of the 66 locomotives were built at Nine Elms, although this particular example was one of those that were built by Dübs & Co in Glasgow (in September 1899). Following Drummond's death, each of the locomotives was equipped with a larger smokebox incorporating a superheater and fitted with a stovepipe chimney, while the cross-water tubes that had been fitted in their fireboxes to increase the heat surface area of the water were removed and the diameter of their cylinders was increased to 19 in. These alterations helped to improve their already excellent performance, so much so in fact that the locomotives continued to be used on express services between Salisbury and Exeter even after the introduction of the larger locomotive designs that ought to have replaced them on these duties, and it was not until 1951 that the first members of the class were withdrawn, by which point they had been relegated to working secondary duties such as services over the North Cornwall Line. No. 30724 survived until 1959, it being withdrawn from service at Guildford shed in May that year and scrapped at Eastleigh Works the following month. *Dave Marriot*

**Left:** Ex-SR Maunsell N15 Class 4-6-0 No. 30770 "Sir Prianus" stands alongside the coaling stage at Basingstoke shed on 1 April 1956. As is illustrated by the piles of ash in the foreground, engine sheds were particularly dirty places at which to work. For staff at sheds that later received diesel or electric traction it must have come as quite a shock to the system, these newer traction types being much cleaner and easier to work with than their steam-powered counterparts. No. 30770 had entered service with the Southern Railway as No. E770 almost 31 years earlier, in June 1925, and had relatively recently been transferred to Basingstoke at the time of this photograph being taken, it previously being based at Stewarts Lane. It would be transferred away from Basingstoke a month later but returned to the shed in September 1962. Within a month of this move, it became the last member of the class left in operation, but a failure soon afterwards meant that it was withdrawn in November 1962. Having spent several months in the scrap line at Eastleigh Works, it was disposed of during February 1963. *Dave Marriot*

**Above:** Rebuilt Bulleid Merchant Navy Class 4-6-2 No. 35005 "Canadian Pacific" leads the "Bournemouth Belle" westwards through Basingstoke on 1 August 1960. Built at Eastleigh Works as part of Order No. 1068, the locomotive had entered service almost 20 years earlier, it being taken into stock as No. 21C5 in December 1941 and initially allocated to Salisbury shed. Following its naming by Mr F W Mottley, the Acting European Manager of Canadian Pacific, at Victoria station on 27 March 1942, the locomotive was transferred to Exmouth Junction in the autumn of that year, remaining there until a move to Nine Elms in August 1948. By this point the wartime black livery that was applied shortly before the locomotive's naming had been replaced with malachite green, which it wore when it was outshopped, and the locomotive had been renumbered, firstly as No. s21C5 then No. 35005. It continued to carry malachite green until February 1950, when it was repainted into BR express blue. After returning to Exmouth Junction in April 1951, a further repaint came in February 1954, this time into BR green, which the locomotive would continue to wear until the end of its BR career. Shortly after this repaint, the locomotive was sent back to Nine Elms in March 1954, while it was rebuilt to a more conventional outline with Walschaerts valve gear at Eastleigh Works in May 1959, and by time that this photograph was taken the locomotive was based at Bournemouth.

Readers will, perhaps, associate the Canadian Pacific name with a railway company rather than a shipping line. It was the Canadian Pacific Railway that established the shipping line of the same name in the late 19th century, this being intended to provide transpacific links between British Columbia and the Far East. Also operating transatlantic services, which carried many immigrants from Europe to Canada, the company continued to carry passengers, freight and mail until the 1970s, when increasing competition from the airline industry prompted it to focus its attentions on bulk container shipping. Latterly known as CP Ships, the company has since been sold to the German-based TUI Group and merged with its Hapag-Lloyd division. *Dave Marriot*

**Above:** Ex-SR Maunsell U Class 2-6-0 No. 31611 heads westwards from Basingstoke with an unfitted freight train on 4 September 1962. No. 31611 was built as part of the first batch of brand-new U Class locomotives at Brighton Works in April 1928, originally being known as No. A611 and later No. 1611. Allocated at the time of this photograph being taken to the nearby Basingstoke shed, it was withdrawn from service at Guildford in October 1963 and was scrapped at Eastleigh Works in January 1964. *Dave Marriot*

**Right:** Rebuilt Bulleid Battle of Britain Class 4-6-2 No. 34071 "601 Squadron" heads a train for Southampton away from Basingstoke on 4 September 1962. Relatively recently having been rebuilt at this point, the locomotive would remain in operation almost until the end of Southern Region steam, it being withdrawn from service in April 1967 and scrapped by John Cashmore Ltd of Newport, Monmouthshire in September 1967. Built at Brighton Works in April 1948 under the auspices of BR as part of Order No. 3383, it had an operational life of less than 15 years and accumulated a total mileage of 782 028 during this time, 437 599 of which were in its original form. The locomotive began its career based at Dover Marine motive power depot, but was not to stay there for long, being transferred to Stewarts Lane in November 1949. There it stayed until June 1955, after which it was returned to Dover for a further four and a half years, this being followed by a move to Nine Elms in December 1960. From August 1964, it was latterly allocated to Eastleigh.

Unusually, for a steam locomotive at least, No. 34071 carried two different names during its career. It was until August 1948 named "615 Squadron". As the first Battle of Britain Class locomotive to be completed for BR, it was decided that it ought to have an official naming ceremony, which was to be undertaken by Group Captain Sir John William Maxwell "Max" Aitken, DSO, DFC, the son of Lord Beaverbrook, who was a director of Express Newspapers and would ensure maximum publicity. Shortly before the ceremony took place, it was realised that a mistake had been made. Aitken was at one point the Commanding Officer of 601 Squadron. Although this qualified to have a locomotive named in its honour, it was not one of the squadrons that was included on the list presented to Mr C Grasemann, the SR Publicity Officer of the time, by the RAF. No. 34071's plates were duly replaced, with the originals being transferred to No. 34082, which was to have been named "66 Squadron", this name being taken by No. 34110. *Dave Marriot*

**Above:** With the Eli Lilly & Company factory visible on the right, ex-SR Bulleid West Country Class No. 34023 "Blackmore Vale" blows off as it approaches Basingstoke on 26 September 1964. Owned by an American pharmaceutical firm, the factory, a prominent feature in many photographs of Basingstoke, was opened in September 1939 just after the outbreak of World War II. During the conflict, its bright white paintwork was replaced with camouflage and the neon sign atop its roof was turned off to avoid attracting the attention of the Luftwaffe. Evidently, this worked: the factory, which was served by a private siding, survived the conflict and remained operational for over 60 years. *Dave Marriot*

**Below:** With what is presumed to be the fireman watching on, heavily weathered rebuilt Bulleid Merchant Navy Class 4-6-2 No. 35008 "Orient Line" is pictured at the head of "The Royal Wessex" near Basingstoke on 5 September 1962. Due to overcrowding, the BR Mark 1 coaches that were used on the service in the 1950s and early 1960s were replaced with the equivalent Bulleid stock, which had a greater capacity, in April 1962. It was for this reason that the later deliveries of Mark 1s to the Southern Region had eight seats within a Second Class compartment rather than six seats as on other regions. Note that the coaches are carrying BR roundels on their lower bodysides. Those used on "The Royal Wessex" were at one point the only Southern Region vehicles to do so. *Dave Marriot*

**Left:** Rebuilt Bulleid Battle of Britain Class 4-6-2 No. 34052 "Lord Dowding" is pictured between Basingstoke and Worting Junction while working a special train on 8 July 1962. Named in honour of Air Chief Marshal Sir Hugh Dowding, a World War I fighter pilot who led Fighter Command from its inception in 1936 until November 1940 and was credited with playing a key role in defeating the plans to invade Britain during World War II, the locomotive was built at Brighton Works as part of Order No. 3213 in December 1946. Originally known as No. 21C152, it was officially named by Lord Dowding himself in a ceremony at Waterloo station on 11 September 1947. Its renumbering into the BR number series came in February 1949, while its SR malachite green livery was replaced with BR green in August 1952. After accumulating 507 986 miles in its original form, the locomotive was rebuilt at Eastleigh Works in September 1958. In this condition it would see almost another nine years of service and travelled a further 428 516 miles before being withdrawn from Salisbury shed, its home since June 1951, upon the end of Southern Region steam in July 1967. The locomotive was one of only six Light Pacifics that received a general repair and boiler change after being rebuilt, but this was not enough to secure it a place in preservation: the locomotive was scrapped by John Cashmore Ltd of Newport, Monmouthshire in February 1968. *Dave Marriot*

**Above:** Seen on the southern outskirts of Basingstoke on 2 September 1962, rebuilt Bulleid Merchant Navy Class 4-6-2 No. 35001 "Channel Packet" demonstrates the capability of the class by making light work of a heavy train consisting of some 13 vehicles. The first of 30 Merchant Navy Class locomotives, No. 35001 was built at Eastleigh Works in February 1941 as part of Order No. 1068, being outshopped as No. 21C1. After its initial testing, it was named in the yard of the Hampshire works on 10 March 1941 by J T C Moore-Brabazon, the Conservative Member of Parliament for Wallasey and Minister of Transport at the time. Further tests followed, the locomotive eventually entering service at Salisbury shed in June 1941. It was at first used on freight traffic, but once the war was over it became clear what it and its classmates were designed for, it reaching a speed of 98 mph while working the "Golden Arrow" on 13 April 1946. After its time on the Eastern Section, it returned to Exmouth Junction, its home since the autumn of 1942, and remained there until January 1957. During this time, the locomotive's appearance was changed on multiple occasions. The peaked casing to its smokebox was replaced with a hood in October 1943, while the locomotive was repainted from malachite green into wartime black in January 1944, it being returned to malachite green after a visit to Eastleigh Works in December 1945. Having gained its BR number in October 1949, the locomotive was painted into BR express blue in December 1950, which it carried until May 1952. It latterly carried BR green. Following its transfer to Stewarts Lane, the locomotive was reallocated to Nine Elms in May 1959. Soon after this move, in August 1959, it was despatched to Eastleigh Works to be rebuilt into the condition in which it is seen here. In this form the locomotive saw a further five years of service, it being withdrawn in November 1964, by which point it was based at Bournemouth. Its scrapping was undertaken by the Slag Reduction Company of Rotherham in November 1964. *Dave Marriot*

**Left:** Rebuilt Bulleid West Country Class 4-6-2 No. 34045 "Ottery St. Mary" passes a building site on the outskirts of Basingstoke on 19 October 1963. Allocated new to Exeter's Exmouth Junction motive power depot in October 1946 as No. 21C145, the locomotive was later based at Salisbury (from April 1951 to June 1951), Brighton (from June 1951 to September 1958), Nine Elms (from September 1958 to February 1959) and Bournemouth (from February 1959 to June 1964). *Dave Marriot*

**Above:** Ex-SR Maunsell S15 Class 4-6-0 No. 30840 leads a lengthy freight train bound for the West of England away from Basingstoke on 19 October 1963. Developed from the design of his H15 and N15 Classes to work heavy freight services such as this, the first S15s were built under the auspices of Urie in the early 1920s. After replacing Urie in 1923, Maunsell modified the design to increase its power output and make it more gauge friendly, enabling the locomotives to be used on the Eastern and Central Sections of the SR network. Built as part of the final batch of S15s, No. 30840 was introduced into service in 1936. Its entire BR career was spent operating out of Feltham depot, from where it was withdrawn in September 1964, being scrapped by P Woods (Shipbreaking) at Queenborough on the Isle of Sheppey later that year. *Dave Marriot*

**Left:** As they neared the end of their careers, the condition of the Bulleid Pacifics was, understandably, allowed to deteriorate, with their once gleaming paintwork being covered in thick layers of grime. Heavily weathered rebuilt Merchant Navy Class 4-6-2 No. 35006 "Peninsular & Oriental S. N. Co." leads a Down West of England express away from Basingstoke on 19 October 1963. The shipping line after which the locomotive was named was founded in the 1820s but was not to become known as the Peninsular & Oriental Steam Navigation Company until it became a limited liability company, incorporated by Royal Charter, in December 1840 in order to attract investors to fund the development of larger ships and the necessary facilities to support the introduction of new mail service between the UK and India. As it won further contracts, the company grew to become the main operator of steam shipping services between Britain and the East; however, its near monopoly was threatened by the opening of the Suez Canal in 1869. Consolidation and modernisation of the fleet followed, ensuring the company's survival into the 20th century, when it merged with the British India Steam Navigation Company and gained a controlling interest in the Orient Line. Further acquisitions followed so that by the mid-1920s the company's fleet amounted to almost 500 vessels and its interests touched almost all parts of the globe. Restructured into different divisions during the 1970s, the P&O name has since disappeared as parts of the business were sold off, its stake in the container shipping operation P&O Nedlloyd being sold to Maersk in 2005, while the company itself was taken over by DP World in 2006. *Dave Marriot*

**Above:** Collett 4900 Class 4-6-0 No. 6923 "Croxteth Hall" puts on a fine display as it hauls an inter-regional express away from Basingstoke on 16 May 1964. Named after the country estate forming the ancestral home of the Molyneux family, which was built around 1575 and set in the West Derby suburb of Liverpool, the locomotive was outshopped from the GWR's Swindon Works in July 1941. After almost a quarter of a century of service, it was withdrawn from Oxford shed in December 1965 and was scrapped by John Cashmore Ltd of Newport, Monmouthshire during May 1966. *Dave Marriot*

**Below:** A stark contrast with the modern factory building on the left, rebuilt Bulleid Merchant Navy Class 4-6-2 No. 35012 "United States Lines" leads a train for the West of England away from Basingstoke on 16 May 1964. Several weeks before this photograph was taken, on 24 April 1964, the locomotive had been used to haul ex-London & North Eastern Railway (LNER) Gresley Class A4 4-6-2 No. 60008 "Dwight D. Eisenhower" from Eastleigh to Southampton Docks in readiness for its export to the USA. In the days that followed it was also used to haul a special train carrying dignitaries from Waterloo to Southampton to witness the presentation of the A4 to the American Railroad Museum at Green Bay, Wisconsin. During his speech thanking BR for the locomotive, the head of the museum indicated that he would also be interested in displaying No. 35012 upon its eventual withdrawal. Unfortunately, nothing more came of this and, having been sold to John Cashmore Ltd of Newport, Monmouthshire, the locomotive was dismantled in October 1967. *Dave Marriot*

**Above:** With one of the residents of the railwayman's cottages looking on and its driver keeping a close eye on the road ahead, rebuilt Bulleid West Country Class 4-6-2 No. 34031 "Torrington" approaches Worting Junction while working a train from Waterloo to the West of England on 2 September 1962. *Dave Marriot*

**Below:** Rebuilt Bulleid Battle of Britain Class 4-6-2 No. 34050 "Royal Observer Corps" heads a "Royal Observer Corps Special Train" away from Worting Junction towards Waterloo on 13 September 1964. Built at Brighton Works in December 1946 as part of the third batch of Bulleid's Light Pacifics (Nos. 21C146–21C170), which were constructed under Order No. 3213, the locomotive entered service as No. 21C150. It was allocated new to Salisbury shed, spending several years there before being transferred to Nine Elms in January 1950, by which point it had been renumbered as No. 34050. The locomotive would remain at the south London shed until March 1951, after which it was allocated to Exmouth Junction (until June 1951) and then, once again, to Salisbury (until November 1960). It was during its second stint at Salisbury, in the summer of 1958, that the locomotive was rebuilt at Eastleigh Works into the form in which it is seen here. After being moved to Bricklayers Arms for a little over a year, the locomotive returned to Nine Elms between October 1961 and August 1964. Whilst there, in a ceremony at Waterloo station on 2 July 1961, it was presented with the Royal Observer Corps' long service medal ribbon by Air Commodore C M Wight-Boycott, Commandant ROC. Taking the form of a plaque, this fitted either side of the locomotive's cab and can be seen just below the cabside number. Shortly before this photograph was taken, the locomotive was reallocated to Eastleigh, from where it was eventually withdrawn in August 1965 after covering 796 814 miles during its 19 years of service. The locomotive was disposed of by the Bird Group at Morriston, Swansea in December 1965. *Dave Marriot*

**Below:** Ex-SR Maunsell Lord Nelson Class 4-6-0 No. 30861 "Lord Anson" leads the Southern Counties Touring Society's "South Western Limited" westwards near Worting Junction on 2 September 1962. The train, which was organised to commemorate the withdrawal of the "Lord Nelsons", was originally advertised to have been hauled from Waterloo to Sidmouth Junction by the class's namesake locomotive, No. 30850; however, this was withdrawn the previous month and by this point only four of the locomotives remained in traffic, the others being Nos. 30856 "Lord St. Vincent", 30857 "Lord Howe" and 30862 "Lord Collingwood". Indeed, it is believed that it was the last time one of the class appeared on a railtour prior to No. 30850 returning to the main line in preservation. No. 30861 was eventually withdrawn at Eastleigh during October 1962, it and No. 30862 being the last two members of the class in service.

Originally intended to address the SR's need for more powerful locomotives, which would be capable of hauling trains weighing up to 500 tons at average speeds of 55 mph over both the Eastern and Western Sections of the SR system, most of the "Lord Nelsons" were only a little over 30 years old at the time of their withdrawal; No. 30850, however, saw 35 years' service. The reason for this was that after it was outshopped from Eastleigh Works in August 1926, No. E850, as it was originally numbered, underwent extensive testing before any further orders were placed.

As the weight restrictions imposed by the railway's civil engineer prevented any enlargement of the two-cylinder designs in operation at the time, the prototype locomotive, which had to have four cylinders in order to meet with the specification, was carefully designed so that its weight was kept to a minimum. High tensile steel was used for the motion, parts that would normally have been left as they were cast were machined to remove excess material, while the frames were made as thin as possible and holes were cut in them to further reduce their weight. Not only this, the locomotive featured a divided drive, with the inside cylinders driving the front coupled axle and the outside ones driving the middle coupled axle, so as to improve weight distribution and reduce hammer blow. Unusually, it also had its cranks set at 135°, which resulted in eight exhaust beats per revolution rather than the usual four, giving a more even draw on the fire and reducing the risk of wheelslip when starting. Another unusual feature of the design was that its fire grate was made up of two separate sections, the rear part being horizontal and the front sloping sharply away to give an area of 33 sq ft, which made it the largest of any British locomotive at the time.

The prototype was, of course, a success. It weighed a little over one ton more than the earlier N15 Class 4-6-0s, but had a tractive effort that was 33% greater, which for a time made it the most powerful locomotive in the country. The encouraging results saw an order placed for an additional ten locomotives (Nos. E851–E860) to be delivered between May 1928 and April 1929, with an order for another ten being placed during 1928. This, however, was later cut to just five locomotives when it was realised that the stock market crash of 1929 would reduce the demand for travel to the Continent.

Ironically, the 500-ton trains for which the locomotives were designed never materialised. They did, however, regularly work trains weighing in excess of 450 tons, including the "Golden Arrow", which linked Victoria with Dover, and the boat trains between Waterloo and Southampton. *Dave Marriot*

**Right:** Rebuilt Bulleid West Country Class 4-6-2 No. 34039 "Boscastle" approaches Worting Junction on 19 April 1960 with a service bound for Waterloo. Built at Brighton Works, the locomotive entered service in September 1946 as No. 21C139. It was initially based at Stewarts Lane and was generally used to work services from Victoria to destinations on the Kent coast, such as the seaside resorts of Margate and Ramsgate or the ports at Dover and Folkestone. Having passed into the ownership of BR, the locomotive became No. 34039 in June 1948. It received its name, which comes from a village on the north coast of Cornwall, at the same time. It was for several months a regular performer on the "Golden Arrow" Pullman service between Victoria and Dover, but November 1948 saw the locomotive transferred to Brighton, from where it worked services along the South coast to Southampton and on to Bournemouth or Salisbury. In August 1949, "Boscastle" became the first member of the West Country Class to receive BR green livery. Another one of the locomotive's claims is that two years later, when Brighton lost its allocation of Bulleid Pacifics, it was one of the three locomotives that were transferred to the Eastern Region for trials, the others being Nos. 34057 "Biggin Hill" and 34065 "Hurricane". Whilst at Stratford, these were used on services from Liverpool Street to Cambridge, Harwich and Norwich, but they did not find favour with local crews, who preferred the newly introduced "Britannias". It was eventually returned to Brighton in March 1952 and remained there for almost seven years, being transferred to Bournemouth in February 1959, by which point the locomotive had been rebuilt. Having covered 466 238 miles since its introduction into traffic, it became due a Heavy General overhaul in November 1958 and was sent to Eastleigh Works to be rebuilt at the same time. It emerged from this in January 1959. Whilst based at Bournemouth, the locomotive was used to work services over the main line from Waterloo to Weymouth, including the "Bournemouth Belle" and "Royal Wessex", and on 19 June 1959 it became the first rebuilt West Country to work over the former S&DJR route towards Bath. It was for a while a regular on the route, but in September 1962 the locomotive was reallocated to Eastleigh. Whilst there it continued to work services over the main line between Waterloo and Bournemouth, including the heavy boat trains originating from Southampton Docks. It remained at Eastleigh until May 1965. After covering 745 508 miles during its career, the locomotive was then withdrawn and sold to Woodham Brothers Ltd of Barry for disposal, but having languished in the South Wales scrapyard for around seven years it was purchased for preservation at the Great Central Railway in Leicestershire. *Dave Marriot*

**Above:** Apart from the electrification of the line and the replacement of the semaphore signalling with colour lights, this scene has changed surprisingly little since the days of steam. Rebuilt Bulleid Merchant Navy Class 4-6-2 No. 35028 "Clan Line" passes Worting Junction with UK Railtours' "Hampshire Pullman" on 6 November 2021. *Rhys Jones*

**Below:** With the Battledown Flyover in the background, rebuilt Bulleid Merchant Navy Class 4-6-2 No. 35009 "Shaw Savill" approaches Worting Junction with an Up West of England express on 18 April 1960. Built under Order No. 1068, the locomotive was outshopped from Eastleigh Works in June 1942 as No. 21C9. Wearing wartime black, it entered traffic at Salisbury shed soon afterwards. It was officially named by Lord Essendon, Chairman of Shaw, Savill & Albion Line, in a ceremony at Victoria station on 30 July 1942. Classmate No. 21C7 was named "Aberdeen Commonwealth" at the same event. The locomotive was repainted into malachite green in November 1946 and, having been renumbered as No. 35009, was given a further repaint, into BR express blue, in August 1949. It remained in this guise until February 1953, when it gained a coat of BR green. Rebuilding came in March 1957, by which point the locomotive had amassed 684 482 miles, and upon the completion of this it was transferred from Salisbury to Exmouth Junction, where it remained until withdrawal in September 1964 having run a total of 1 127 452 miles. The locomotive was subsequently sold to Woodham Brothers Ltd of Barry and was eventually purchased for preservation in the 1980s.

The shipping line after which the locomotive was named was formed in 1858 to facilitate trade between Britain and New Zealand. It was merged in 1882 with the Albion Shipping Company, which also carried cargo, mail and passengers to and from New Zealand, after which it became known as the Shaw, Savill & Albion Line. Taking joint control of Aberdeen Line in 1905, the company later began to operate to and from Australia. Having purchased Aberdeen Line outright in 1932, the company was itself taken over in 1933 by Furness Withy, although it retained its own identity. After suffering heavy losses during World War II, the company embarked upon a major expansion programme, its fleet reaching a peak of 33 vessels in the late 1960s. Not long after this, though, it became clear that it could no longer compete with the airlines for passenger traffic, which led to its remaining passenger ships being scrapped in 1975. Its last cargo ship, meanwhile, was sold in 1986. The company was eventually taken over by Hamburg Sud. *Dave Marriot*

**Below:** Easily recognised from its extended smoke deflectors, which were fitted prior to its participation in the 1948 Locomotive Exchanges, ex-SR Bulleid West Country Class 4-6-2 No. 34006 "Bude" is pictured heading a train in the Up direction over the Battledown Flyover on 19 April 1960. Also unusual in being the only West Country Class locomotive named after a location in Cornwall to receive an individual crest, the rest carrying the Cornish Coat of Arms, the locomotive was outshopped from Brighton Works in August 1945 and was initially based at Exmouth Junction motive power depot. It was named by Councillor John Hallett, Chairman of the Stratton and Bude Urban District Council, in a ceremony at Bude station on 1 November 1945. At first it also wore the Cornish Coat of Arms; however, the local borough created its own in the years that followed, which led to a pair of new enamelled crests being fitted to the locomotive in the early 1950s, by which point it had been renumbered into the BR number series and repainted into BR green. At the time that this photograph was taken the locomotive would have been based at Nine Elms, it having been transferred there in March 1951. Although the locomotive was not one of those that were selected to be rebuilt, it eventually received a cut down tender like those that were paired with the rebuilt locomotives in August 1961. It ran with this for almost six years before being withdrawn from service at Salisbury in March 1967. With an operational life of almost 22 years, "Bude" achieved the highest mileage out of all the Light Pacifics, covering a total of 1 099 338 miles during this time. The only other Light Pacifics to achieve more than a million miles in service were Nos. 34001 "Exeter" and 34002 "Salisbury". No. 34006 was scrapped by John Cashmore Ltd of Newport, Monmouthshire in September 1967.
*Dave Marriot*

**Above:** Seen from a similar vantage point to where the photo opposite was taken but almost six decades on, rebuilt Bulleid Merchant Navy Class 4-6-2 No. 35018 "British India Line" heads away from Worting Junction towards Southampton with a Railway Touring Company charter from Victoria to Weymouth on 6 July 2019.

One of 11 Merchant Navies to survive into preservation, the locomotive was built at the SR's Eastleigh Works in 1945 and entered service in May that year. It differed from the rest of the class in its coupled wheels being fabricated, although these were soon replaced with the standard cast type. Originally known as No. 21C18, it was initially allocated to Nine Elms motive power depot. Indeed, but for a brief spell at Bournemouth in the autumn of 1960, it spent most of its BR life at the south London shed, eventually being withdrawn from there in August 1964. Officially named at Waterloo station on 13 December 1945 by Mr A J Lang, the Managing Director of the shipping line after which it was named, the locomotive was given its BR number in May 1948 at the same time as being fitted with a Flaman speed recorder and a new wedge-shaped cab. In another claim to fame, the locomotive was the first of the class to lose its air-smoothed casing, it emerging from Eastleigh Works in its rebuilt form in February 1956. Aside from the lack of handrails on its smoke deflectors, which were added soon afterwards, the locomotive differed from later rebuilds in a number of ways: its front sandbox fillers were positioned higher up than on other examples; the feed pipes to its clack valves included a right-angled bend, whereas those on its classmates were straight; and the blower and brake ejector pipes were curved above the level of the nameplate, rather than at the junction of the smokebox and the boiler barrel.

Having been sold to Woodham Brothers Ltd of Barry upon its withdrawal from service, the locomotive was moved to South Wales in March 1965. It remained there for some 15 years before being moved to the Mid Hants Railway for restoration. After changing hands a number of times, it was steamed for the first time in over 50 years in November 2016 and is nowadays based at Carnforth in the North-West of England. *Rhys Jones*

# CHAPTER 2
## THE WEST OF ENGLAND LINE

From Worting Junction, we take the West of England Line through Salisbury to Exeter, a distance of around 122 miles. Providing a stark contrast with the busy line through the densely populated south-western suburbs of London that was the focus of the first part of our journey, this next stage of our route passes mostly through rural countryside interspersed with small towns and villages, many of which were served by wayside stations (shown on the accompanying maps) that were closed during the 1960s under the orders of Doctor Richard Beeching, the Chairman of the BR Board at the time. The first 40 miles or so of the route are dominated by the chalk downlands of northern Hampshire and the southern edge of Salisbury Plain, land which was once used for sheep grazing but became more commonly associated with the growing of crops, such as wheat and barley, after World War II. The line dissects the landscape via a combination of deep cuttings and high embankments, which help to minimise its gradients. It is far from flat, however. After passing through Oakley, the line runs downhill most of the way to what used to be known as Andover Junction, a once important station where the West of England Line met the former Midland & South Western Junction Railway route linking Cheltenham, Swindon and Southampton. Continuing westwards, the line then climbs for around seven miles, with gradients of up to 1 in 165, to Grateley, after which it falls downgrade all the way into Salisbury, which is by far the largest centre of population along the route and remains an important location on the railway network, though, its facilities are much reduced in comparison to what they once were.

### *Salisbury*

In the latter days of steam, visitors to Salisbury would have found an extensive goods yard at the eastern end of the station, opposite which was the junction for the Market House branch and Salisbury East signal box, one of three signal boxes that controlled movements in the station area, the others being Salisbury West and Salisbury 'C' signal boxes. The station itself is much the same as it was then, though, there are fewer platforms in use nowadays, the track layout has been rationalised and, of course, the infrastructure installed to support the operation of steam locomotives is long gone. Further freight handling facilities would have been found to the north and west of the station, the former (Fisherton Sidings) being located on the land that was previously occupied by the terminus of the Wiltshire, Somerset & Weymouth Railway (WS&WR) route from Westbury, which was operated by the GWR. Like the line from Reading to Basingstoke, the WS&WR was originally built to broad gauge. It was not until 1878, by which point it had been converted to standard gauge, that a connection to the adjacent LSWR line was installed to ease the transfer of goods. Through passenger services were later introduced, but it was not until September 1932 that the Brunellian terminus ceased to be used for passenger traffic. The trainshed was subsequently demolished. The station buildings, however, survived and were later granted Grade II listed status. As well as its own station and goods facilities, the WS&WR had its own motive power depot in the town. This was originally located on the south side of the terminus but was demolished around the turn of the 20th century to make way for the expansion of the neighbouring LSWR station. Its replacement, which was built on the north side of the line, was closed by BR in November 1950. The much larger ex-LSWR facility opposite it, which incorporated a ten-road engine shed and a 70 ft turntable, remained operational right up until the end of Southern Region steam. Neither survives.

### *The Salisbury & Yeovil Railway*

Continuing westwards from Salisbury, we join the route of the Salisbury & Yeovil Railway (S&YR), which paralleled the WS&WR as far as Wilton before continuing across country through Gillingham, Templecombe and Sherborne to the market town of Yeovil. Operated from the outset by the LSWR, which later took it over, this was opened in 1859–60 after an earlier proposal put forward by the LSWR to provide a direct connection from Basingstoke to Salisbury and thence to Yeovil and Exeter failed to come to fruition. The number of new railway schemes that were approved during the railway mania of the 1840s was such that this caused an economic depression. The LSWR was, therefore, unable to raise the funds required for the construction of the proposed line and the powers were allowed to lapse (suggestions that the extension to Exeter should have followed a coastal route from Dorchester are cited as another reason for the plan failing to progress). The first part of this route (described above) was eventually opened in the mid-to-late 1850s, however, with the line from Yeovil to Exeter opening within a matter of weeks of the S&YR's completion. A connection from what later become Exeter Central to the GWR station at Exeter St Davids was completed in 1862.

Like the section east of Salisbury, this part of the West of England Line runs mostly through rural countryside, the difficult terrain that was encountered meaning that most of the important towns in the area had to be bypassed when the line was built, with the multiple river valleys that punctuate the upland areas formed from chalk, limestone or Upper Greensand, giving it something of a switchback profile, the downhill sections of which were conducive to high-speed running during the days of steam. When heading westwards from Salisbury, trains face a stiff climb of 1 in 115 for around a mile and a quarter, after which the rising gradients ease as the railway follows the valleys of the meandering River Nadder and its tributary the River Sem as far as the summit at Semley. As we progress further, the large arable fields that dominated the landscape for the first 20 miles or so after Salisbury give way to areas of woodland, hedgerows and smaller lowland pastures used for dairy farming, while the line descends downhill for four miles at gradients of 1 in 100, 1 in 114 and 1 in 130 to Gillingham before climbing once again, with a short section of 1 in 440 being followed by a mile at 1 in 300 and a then a mile at 1 in 100 to the summit at the eastern portal of Buckhorn Weston Tunnel, which provides passage through a ridge made up of Corallian limestone. Upon exiting the tunnel, the line continues downgrade at a ruling gradient of 1 in 90 for several miles across the clays of the Vale of Blackmore, an area of natural beauty at the foot of a chalk escarpment. A short section of level line precedes a further climb through Templecombe, which is where the West of England Line intersected the former S&DJR route from Bath to Bournemouth.

### Templecombe

Hard as it is to imagine now, Templecombe used to be home to a thriving railway community. When Dave visited the village in the late 1950s and 1960s, he would've found not only a sizeable station on the West of England Line but also a halt on the former S&DJR route, known as Templecombe Lower Platform, alongside which there was a small motive power depot equipped with a 50 ft turntable and a two-road engine shed that housed some of the locomotives that were used on the services to Bath and Bournemouth. After the small shed in the upper yard was closed in the 1930s, this was also home to the locomotives used on shunting and station pilot duties. It too was closed after the Beeching axe fell on the former S&DJR route in March 1966. The upper station, which was once a major interchange, served by all except a small number of express services, shut at the same time. It has since been reopened, though, its facilities are much reduced from what they once were.

To the west of Templecombe, the line continues to climb for around a mile and a half to pass over a ridge of Jurassic limestone. It then falls almost constantly for the next nine miles as it passes through Milborne Port and Sherborne to follow the valley of the River Yeo as far as Yeovil, where the river turns to the north to head for the Bristol Channel.

### Yeovil

Like Templecombe, Yeovil used to be an important railway centre. Until the late 1960s, it was served by no fewer than three stations – Yeovil Junction, Yeovil Town and Yeovil Pen Mill – the first of these three being situated on the West of England Line around two miles south of the town near the hamlet of Stoford. It was connected to the more centrally located Yeovil Town and the motive power depot that stood alongside the station via a curve to the route taken by the S&YR, which left what later became the main line to Exeter to the east of Yeovil Junction, crossed over the former WS&WR line from Westbury to Weymouth and then ran alongside this for several miles before turning westwards to reach its terminus on the south side of the town, while a direct connection to Yeovil Pen Mill (on what was originally the WS&WR) was installed during World War II to enable trains to be easily diverted in the event of bomb damage.

Progressing ever further westwards, as we leave Yeovil Junction behind the line starts to climb once again in order to cross another limestone ridge, with the summit being reached around a mile and a quarter beyond Sutton Bingham. An undulating stretch follows, then after crossing the River Parrett there is another climb (mainly at 1 in 80) as the line passes through Crewkerne. From Hewish, it then drops downgrade for a distance of around 13 miles as it runs along the valley of the River Axe, passing the site of the United Dairies milk factory that was once a major source of traffic at Chard Junction, to reach Axminster, which was where for many years holidaymakers bound for the seaside resort of Lyme Regis changed trains. It was for this reason that the majority of passenger services stopped at Axminster during the 1950s and 1960s. For those that didn't, the long descent from Hewish could be used to build up speed ahead of the climb to Honiton Tunnel, which is mostly at a gradient of 1 in 80 for some seven miles, the only real respite from this being a short section of 1 in 300 marking the site of the former Seaton Junction, another once busy station that was closed (along with the branch to Seaton) in March 1966. With the summit of the line being situated just beyond its western portal, the sight of Honiton Tunnel, the longest tunnel on the former LSWR network, would no doubt have come as relief to the crews of steam locomotives, particularly firemen who would have been given quite a workout as they sought to maintain a healthy supply of steam. From there, it is downhill almost all the way to Exeter, the only exception being another undulating stretch where the line leaves the Otter Valley and passes through Feniton, which was where the branch to Sidmouth left the main line.

### Exeter

The approach to Exeter is marked by the branch from Exmouth trailing in from the south at the appropriately titled Exmouth Junction. The busiest of all the West of England Line's branches, this is now the only one to survive. Exmouth Junction used to be the site of a marshalling yard, where freight trains were reformed before goods could continue on the way to their destination. As well as this, there once was a carriage and wagon repair facility here, not to mention a concrete manufacturing plant and, of course, Exmouth Junction motive power depot. The Southern Region's main motive power depot in the West Country, this was modernised by the SR in the late 1920s and boasted an engine shed with 13 roads of 270 ft in length, a 70 ft turntable and a mechanical coaling tower. At its peak, it was home to over 120 locomotives, which were used to work services over the main line towards Waterloo and over secondary routes across the West Country, from east Devon to north Cornwall. Having been transferred to the Western Region in 1963, the depot's allocation of Bulleid Pacifics and other ex-SR designs was replaced by an array of tank engines, mostly BR Standards. It was closed to steam in June 1965 but continued to service diesel locomotives until February 1967, after which the depot was demolished.

From Exmouth Junction it is only a short distance to Exeter Central, which is another location that has changed considerably over the years. Once a bustling station with trains from Waterloo being split into smaller portions prior to continuing to various destinations in the West of England and the reverse procedure taking place with trains heading in the opposite direction, locomotive changes being carried out, shunting taking place in the adjacent goods yard and trains being banked up the 1-in-37 gradient from Exeter St Davids, Exeter Central is now a shadow of its former self. As with many places along the West of England Line, the track layout has been heavily rationalised in the name of modernisation. Fortunately, Exeter St Davids, the main station in the city, and its surroundings have not been as badly affected. Even the motive power depot at the rear of the station has survived, albeit much modernised, to house the DMUs that are now used on the local services in the Exeter area.

# THE WEST OF ENGLAND LINE AND ITS CONNECTIONS

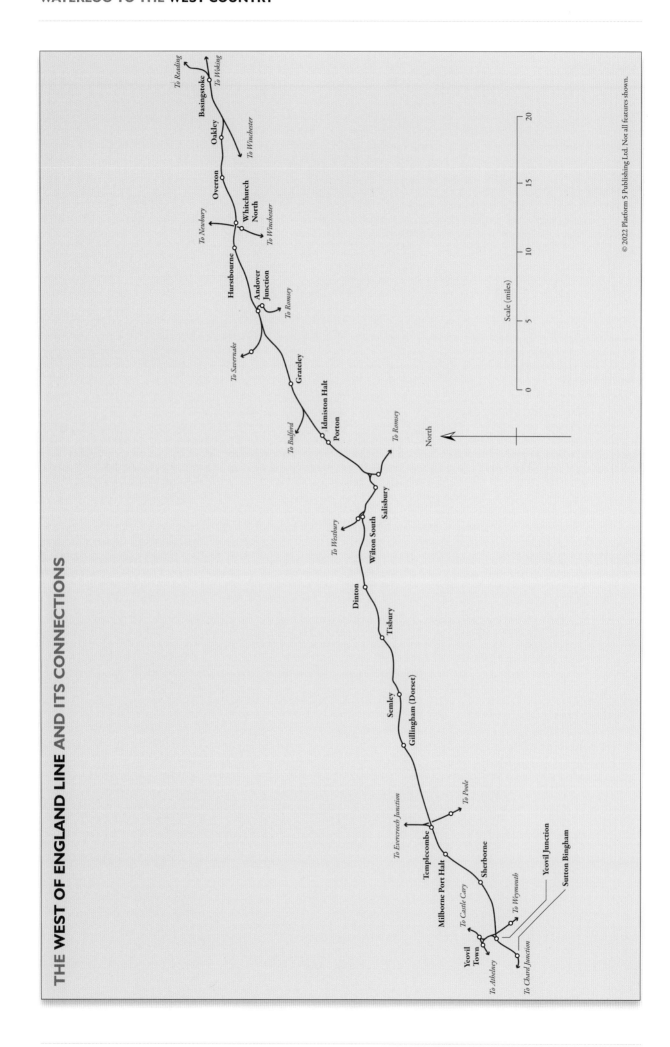

# THE WEST OF ENGLAND LINE AND ITS CONNECTIONS

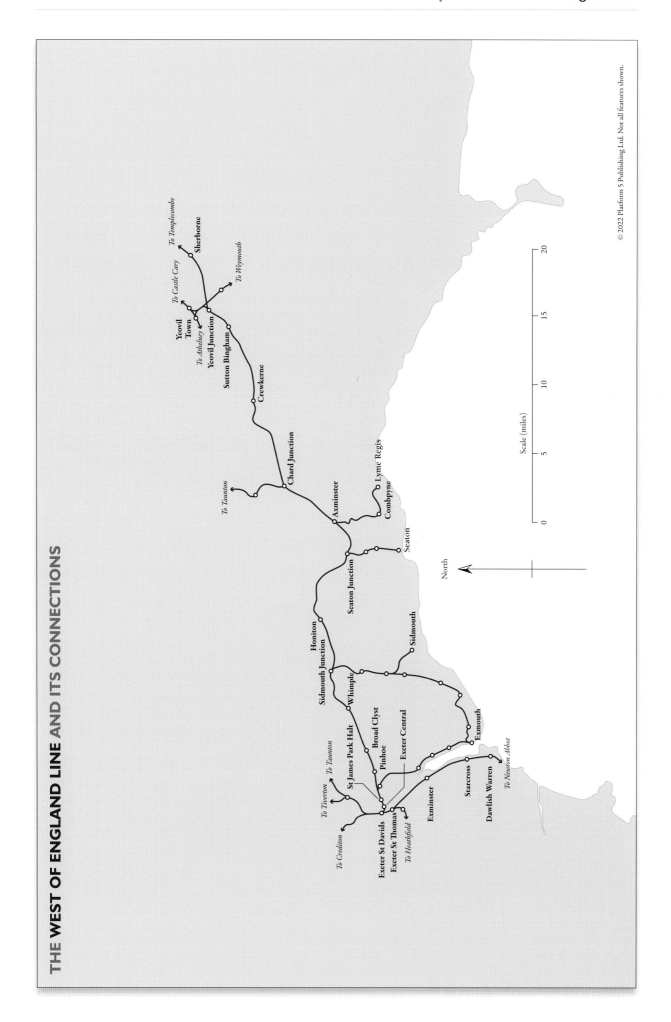

Sherborne
To Templecombe
To Castle Cary
Yeovil Town
To Abbetbury
Yeovil Junction
To Weymouth
Sutton Bingham
Crewkerne
Chard Junction
To Taunton
Axminster
Lyme Regis
Combpyne
Seaton
Seaton Junction
Honiton
Sidmouth Junction
Sidmouth
Whimple
Broad Clyst
Pinhoe
Exeter Central
St James Park Halt
To Tiverton
To Taunton
Exeter St Davids
Exeter St Thomas
To Crediton
To Heathfield
Exminster
Exmouth
Starcross
Dawlish Warren
To Newton Abbot

North

Scale (miles)
0     5     10     15     20

**Above:** Rebuilt Bulleid Merchant Navy Class 35028 "Clan Line" takes the Salisbury line away from Worting Junction on 10 August 2019 as it hauls the outward leg of UK Railtours' "Atlantic Coast Express" railtour from Waterloo to Exeter St Davids. Apart from the locomotive's highly polished finish, air pipes and overhead electrification warning notices, and also the presence of its Mark 2 support coach, the scene would have been little different in the 1960s. *Rhys Jones*

**Above:** Ex-SR Maunsell N15 Class 4-6-0 No. 30448 "Sir Tristram" rests in the company of BR Standard Class 4MT 2-6-0 No. 76008 at Salisbury shed on 1 April 1956. Built at Eastleigh Works in May 1925, No. 30448 was one of the ten N15 Class locomotives that adopted the numbers of earlier Urie G14 Class locomotives and acquired the tenders that were paired with these. After spending the entirety of its BR career based at Salisbury, it was withdrawn in August 1960. The shed, a ten-road structure situated on the south side of the line to the west of Salisbury station, was closed shortly before the end of Southern Region steam. *Dave Marriot*

**Above:** Organised as a celebration of the final days of steam on the Southern Region, the RCTS's "Farewell to Southern Steam" railtour on 18 June 1967 saw a pair of Bullied West Country Class Pacifics, Nos. 34023 "Blackmore Vale" and 34108 "Wincanton", rostered to work the train from Weymouth to Salisbury via Southampton Central. Both devoid of their smokebox numberplates and nameplates, the pair are pictured shortly before coming off the train at Salisbury, where they were replaced by rebuilt Bulleid Merchant Navy Class 4-6-2 No. 35013 "Blue Funnel" for the last leg of the tour back to Waterloo. No. 34023 survived into preservation, but No. 34108 was not so fortunate. This was reputedly its last passenger working, it being withdrawn soon afterwards and sold to J Buttigieg of Newport, Monmouthshire for scrapping. *Rhys Jones*

**Above:** Rebuilt Bulleid West Country Class 4-6-2 No. 34008 "Padstow" stands at Salisbury in September 1965. *Rhys Jones*

**Above:** Rebuilt Bulleid Merchant Navy Class 4-6-2 No. 35018 "British India Line" is pictured just to the west of Tisbury on 9 July 2019 with 1Z92, the 08.45 Victoria–Yeovil Pen Mill leg of The Railway Touring Company's annual railtour to celebrate the anniversary of the end of steam on the Southern Region. It is not immediately obvious from the angle at which this photograph was taken, but this part of the line was reduced to single-track status after the route west of Salisbury came under the control of BR's Western Region in 1963. When Dr Beeching's The Development of the Major Railway Trunk Routes report was published in February 1965 it revealed that the Western Region's other route from London to the South-West, the former GWR main line from Paddington, had been chosen for development, this being seen to provide the best means by which the principal traffic flows could be concentrated and to connect all the major population centres involved. The former LSWR route was duly rationalised, with some of the intermediate stations being closed and most of the route being reduced to single track with crossing loops at certain locations. Double track was, however, retained between Salisbury and Wilton, Templecombe and Sherborne, and Pinhoe and Exeter. To increase flexibility, the second line between Sherborne and Yeovil Junction was quickly reinstated, while a dynamic passing loop of several miles in length was opened at Axminster in 2009. A number of stations have since also been reopened. *Rhys Jones*

**Left:** The same locomotive is seen a couple of miles further westwards on the final part of the climb to Semley summit at West Hatch with a similar working from Victoria to Weymouth, which it would haul as far as Yeovil, on 9 July 2021. *Rhys Jones*

**Above:** Rebuilt Bulleid Merchant Navy Class 4-6-2 No. 35028 "Clan Line" approaches the former level crossing on the outskirts of Semley, now a foot crossing, while working 1Z82, the 08.46 Victoria–Sherborne, on 18 August 2021. Titled "The John Farrow Salute", this tour was organised by UK Railtours as a celebration of the life of the company's founder, who passed away in 2020. While the train was serviced at Yeovil Junction its passengers were invited to attend a memorial service at Sherborne Abbey.

Semley station was sited around a mile to the west of this location. Opened in May 1859, this was one of ten intermediate stations between Salisbury and Exeter that were closed after this part of our route was taken over by BR's Western Region in the early 1960s. Given the size of the rural Wiltshire village, its closure should have come as no big surprise. Its main source of traffic was people travelling to and from Shaftesbury, approximately three miles away, who could just as easily travel to the station at Gillingham. *Rhys Jones*

**Above:** BR Standard Class 5MT 4-6-0 No. 73096 leads a Steam Dreams charter from Clapham Junction to Exeter St Davids westwards at Buckhorn Weston, between Gillingham and Templecombe, on 6 July 2003. Although this was not one of the locomotives allocated to the Southern Region during BR days, it was at this time a relatively regular sight on charter trains across the South and West of England, being based along with the stock it is hauling at the Mid Hants Railway. Built at Derby Works in November 1955, it in fact spent its BR career operating over the London Midland and Western Regions, it initially being allocated to Patricroft motive power depot, near Manchester. It was transferred to Shrewsbury in September 1958 and, as was the custom for Class 5 locomotives allocated to the Western Region, while there it was repainted into BR green livery. In June 1962, it moved on again, this time to Gloucester Barnwood depot. After almost two years there, in April 1964 it was reallocated to the nearby Gloucester shed, which remained its home until November 1964. It was then transferred back to the London Midland Region, being based at Wolverhampton's Oxley depot until March 1965, then at Nuneaton (until June 1965), Croes Newydd (until July 1965) and latterly at Patricroft, from where it was withdrawn from service in November 1967. It was subsequently sold to Woodham Brothers Ltd of Barry and having been delivered to the South Wales scrapyard in February 1968 remained there until July 1985. *Rhys Jones*

**Right:** To celebrate the 50th anniversary of the end of Southern Region steam on 9 July 2017, UK Railtours organised a special train, titled "The Waterloo Sunset", from Waterloo to Yeovil Junction using the Merchant Navy Locomotive Preservation Society's rebuilt Bulleid Merchant Navy Class 4-6-2, No. 35028 "Clan Line". Running as 1Z68, the train's return working, the 17.40 Yeovil Junction–Waterloo, is seen here as it bursts out of Buckhorn Weston Tunnel as it heads back towards London. *Rhys Jones*

**Left:** The area above the western portal of Buckhorn Weston Tunnel makes an excellent vantage point from which to watch trains towards Waterloo tackle the 1-in-90 gradient here. Nearing the summit of the short climb, rebuilt Bullied Merchant Navy Class 4-6-2 No. 35028 "Clan Line" takes this in its stride as it works the return leg of UK Railtours' "John Farrow Salute", the 16.55 Sherborne–Victoria, on 18 August 2021. *Rhys Jones*

**Above:** Adams Class G6 0-6-0T No. 30274 is found resting at the former S&DJR shed at Templecombe on 31 March 1956. Situated on the north side of the West of England Line alongside the much-mourned route from Bath Green Park to Bournemouth West, the small shed, opened in 1877, consisted of a two-road dead-end depot building, which was built in 1951 to replace an earlier timber-built structure. It also had turntable of 50 ft in diameter, plus the usual servicing facilities. Built at the LSWR's Nine Elms Works in February 1898, the G6 was sent to Templecombe in August 1950, along with classmate No. 30277, to shunt the yards there. No. 30277 was transferred elsewhere in January 1951, but No. 30274 remained at Templecombe until February 1959. It was withdrawn from service at Bournemouth during the October of the following year and within a month of this it had been cut up at Eastleigh Works. At the time of its withdrawal, it was one of the last five members of the class to remain in service with BR. Interestingly, the G6s represented Adams' only 0-6-0T design. *Dave Marriot*

**Above:** Carrying the identity of long-lost Bulleid Battle of Britain Class 4-6-2 No. 34052 "Lord Dowding", which was scrapped by Woodham Brothers Ltd of Barry in May 1965, rebuilt Bulleid West Country Class 4-6-2 No. 34046 "Braunton" passes Milborne Port with 1Z67, the 09.00 Waterloo–Yeovil Junction leg of The Railway Touring Company's "End of Southern Steam" charter, on 8 July 2017. From Yeovil, a Class 33 diesel locomotive would take the train forward to Weymouth. No. 34046 would then work the return to Waterloo via Bournemouth.

 Having been reduced to being an unstaffed halt in November 1961, the station serving the village of Milborne Port, which was several miles away, was closed in March 1967. Its main station building, on the Down side of the line, survives in private ownership. *Rhys Jones*

**Above:** With a member of staff hitching a lift on one of the tender footsteps, ex-SR Maunsell U Class 2-6-0 No. 31794 is pictured at Yeovil Town motive power depot, which was sited a short distance away from the main Waterloo–Exeter line adjacent to Yeovil Town station, on 31 March 1956. Built as a K Class 2-6-4T by Armstrong Whitworth in 1925, the locomotive was rebuilt as a U Class at Eastleigh Works in June 1928 and at the time of this photograph being taken was resident at Yeovil Town. But for the period between March 1950 and January 1951 when it was based at Reading South, the locomotive had hitherto spent the entirety of its BR career at the depot. In September 1958, however, it was transferred to Eastleigh and was withdrawn from service there in June 1963. The locomotive was scrapped at Eastleigh Works later that same year. The shed, which was opened by the LSWR in 1860, outlasted it by several years, being closed by BR's Western Region in June 1965. Largely hidden by the coal stack, the adjacent station was closed to passengers in October 1966 but remained open for freight and parcels traffic until March 1967. *Dave Marriot*

**Above:** Rebuilt Bulleid Merchant Navy Class 4-6-2 No. 35018 "British India Line" is turned at Yeovil Junction on 9 July 2021. Built by Cowans Sheldon of Carlisle in 1947, the 70 ft turntable here remained in situ beyond the end of Southern steam in 1967, possibly only because of the difficultly in removing it, and continued to see occasional use turning items of on-track plant and steam locomotives that had worked charter trains into the area. In the early 1990s, however, talks were raised regarding its removal and relocation to a heritage railway, which would've made Yeovil much less attractive as a destination for steam-hauled charters, so the South West Main Line Steam Company was set up to secure its future. The organisation also took on the disused island platform alongside and has since developed the site to help encourage the operation of more main line steam, rebuilt approximately half a mile of the GWR's Clifton Maybank branch, which was closed in 1937, and made the adjacent transfer shed (now the only structure of its kind to survive in its original location) into a museum. *Rhys Jones*

**Below:** Nearing the end of its BR career, rebuilt Bulleid Merchant Navy Class 4-6-2 No. 35009 "Shaw Savill" is seen near Yeovil Junction with a westbound express on 2 June 1963. As detailed earlier, upon its withdrawal the locomotive was sold to Woodham Brothers Ltd, which helped to ensure its survival. The South Wales scrap merchant prioritised the processing of rolling stock, meaning that railway preservationists were able to secure the futures of many of the steam locomotives that it purchased. No. 35009 was one of the last 20 locomotives to leave the yard. It was initially moved to Brighton and was to form one of the exhibits in the railway museum that was to be created in the former Pullman sheds at Preston Park. This idea failed to progress, however, and the locomotive has since had several homes. It is yet to steam in preservation. *Dave Marriot*

**Right:** BR Riddles Standard Class 5MT 4-6-0 No. 73096 leads a Steam Dreams "Cathedrals Express" charter from Clapham Junction to Exeter St Davids westwards away from Yeovil Junction and up the 1-in-150 gradient towards Sutton Bingham on 6 July 2003. *Rhys Jones*

**Below:** Rebuilt Bulleid West Country Class 4-6-2 No. 34027 "Taw Valley" heads east at Winsham, between Chard Junction and Crewkerne, on 18 October 1992 with the return working of "The South Western Limited", a railtour from Waterloo to Exeter Central organised by Flying Scotsman Services, Network SouthEast and the Steam Locomotive Operators' Association. Built at Brighton Works in April 1946 under Order No. 2561, the locomotive was initially allocated to Ramsgate to work services between London and the South-East but was transferred to Exmouth Junction in January 1948. Having been renumbered from No. 21C127 to No. 34027 in July 1948, it gained its name in December 1951, this being taken from the valley of a river that rises on Dartmoor and empties into Bideford Bay. Its original SR malachite green livery was replaced with BR green at around the same time. In September 1957, after accumulating 503 085 miles in service, the locomotive became the second of the Light Pacifics to be rebuilt at Eastleigh Works under the instructions of R G Jarvis. Upon its release it was transferred to Bricklayers Arms motive power depot in south London. It was not to stay there for long, however, returning to Ramsgate in February 1958. After another year or so of being based at the Kent coast, it was sent back to Bricklayers Arms in May 1959, then to Brighton in May 1961. The locomotive was latterly based at Salisbury shed, from where it was withdrawn in August 1964 with a total mileage of 764 316. It was subsequently sold to Woodham Brothers Ltd and was moved to Barry in December 1964, spending some 15 years in the South Wales scrapyard before being moved to the North Yorkshire Moors Railway in April 1980 for restoration. Having been moved to the Severn Valley Railway, the locomotive was steamed for the first time in preservation in 1987 and re-entered service the following year. It returned to the main line in 1988 and in September 1992, as part of the celebrations marking the 25th anniversary of the Bournemouth line's electrification, became the first steam locomotive to work a train out of Waterloo since the end of Southern Region steam in July 1967. *Rhys Jones*

**Above:** Ex-LSWR 0415 Class 4-4-2T No. 30583, one of three Adams "Radial Tanks" that were used for many years to work services over the Lyme Regis branch, stands at Axminster during March 1956.

A development of Adams' 46 Class 4-4-0s, the locomotives, 71 of which were built for the LSWR by various outside contractors between 1882 and 1885, were designed to work suburban services in and around London. They performed their duties very well and, in fact, Adams was so pleased with them that he had the 12 46 Class locos rebuilt as Atlantics, so apart from the location of their safety valves they were similar in appearance to the 0415s. The introduction of newer designs, such as the Adams T1 and Drummond M7 0-4-4Ts in the 1890s, resulted in the locomotives being displaced from the London area, although some stayed on to work less demanding duties. The intervention of the First World War meant that the locomotives survived longer than might have otherwise been the case, but by 1930 increasing electrification meant that all but a couple of the 30 0415 Class locomotives that passed into the ownership of the SR in 1923 had been withdrawn. The two that were left were those that were used on the Lyme Regis branch in Dorset (Nos. 0125 and 0520).

Opened in 1903, the branch was worked for the first three years of its existence by a pair of former LBSCR "Terrier" 0-6-0Ts. These were then replaced by more powerful Adams O2 0-4-4Ts, which were better suited to the branch's steep gradients; however, the tight curvature of the line caused these to suffer from excessive wear, including twisted frames. Its light axle loading also meant that the O2s were not allowed to have their water tanks filled to capacity. It was subsequently found that the Adams "Radials" were well suited to the branch, although these too effectively had to have their water capacity reduced, and so a number of locos were transferred to Exmouth Junction in 1913 to replace the O2s. Trials using former LBSCR Stroudley Class D1 0-4-2Ts and an SECR Wainwright P Class 0-6-0T during the decade that followed proved unsuccessful, so the ageing 4-4-2Ts were given an overhaul at Eastleigh Works, which saw them renumbered as Nos. 3125 and 3520. By 1946, however, the SR found itself desperately in need of additional motive power to work the branch.

Fortunately, a third member of the 0415 Class survived in private ownership. Having been declared surplus to requirements by the LSWR, No. 0488 had been sold to the Ministry of Munitions in 1917 for use at Ridham Salvage Depot in Sittingbourne, Kent and then a couple of years later to Colonel Stephens for operation on the East Kent Railway (EKR), which linked Shepherdswell with Richborough Port, to become EKR No. 5. By 1946, the locomotive had been out of use for some time but remained intact and the SR negotiated its purchase for £800. It was then given an overhaul at Eastleigh Works and, having been renumbered once more – as No. 3488, joined its classmates in the South-West. The trio were transferred to British Railways shortly afterwards, in January 1948, No. 3125 becoming No. 30582; No. 3488, No. 30583; and No. 3520, No. 30584.

The locomotive, which was built by Neilson & Co in 1885, would remain in operation for a further five years after this photograph was taken, it eventually being withdrawn in July 1961, after which it passed into preservation at the fledgling Bluebell Railway. It was chosen over its two classmates because it still had an Adams (rather than a Drummond) boiler and was therefore the closest of the three to being in original condition. Following an unsuccessful attempt to replace the locomotives with former GWR Collett 1400 Class 0-4-2Ts in 1958, they were eventually succeeded by BR Ivatt Class 2MT 2-6-2Ts, although this was only possible because some of the sharp curves had been eased when track renewals took place on the branch in 1959. The 2MTs were themselves replaced by DMUs from November 1963. *Dave Marriot*

**Above:** With the bridge that carried the Lyme Regis branch over the West of England Main Line in the background, ex-LSWR Adams 0415 Class 4-4-2T No. 30582 accelerates a two-coach train away from Axminster on 18 May 1959. The locomotive, which was built by Robert, Stephenson & Co of Newcastle in 1885, was withdrawn from traffic at Exmouth Junction just over two years after this photograph was taken, in July 1961, with a total mileage of 2 070 918. It was scrapped at Eastleigh Works during March of the following year. *Dave Marriot*

**Below:** One of the main features of the six-mile branch between Axminster and Lyme Regis was Cannington Viaduct, which was by far the largest structure to be built on a light railway in Britain. Measuring 203 yards long, it featured ten elliptical arches of 50 ft span and 92 ft in height, and was built using an aerial ropeway, from which liquid concrete was poured into shuttering, with pre-cast concrete blocks being cast into the top of the piers to support the timber framework that was used in the construction of the arches. These and the spandrels also featured pre-cast components. While the viaduct was being built, the west end settled. It was stabilised by constructing a diaphragm wall and a jack arch within the third arch from the west end of the viaduct. Built out of pale cream bricks so as to blend in with the rest of the structure, these were braced using bits of old rail. Ex-LSWR Adams 0415 Class 4-4-2T No. 30583 leads a train for Lyme Regis off the viaduct on 18 May 1959. *Dave Marriot*

**Above:** Ex-SR Maunsell Class S15 4-6-0 No. 30832 is pictured heading west at Seaton Junction on 16 May 1959. The lines to the right head to the branch platform and on to the seaside town after which the station was named a little over four miles away, while the bridge in the distance carried a footpath across the station site. A product of the SR's Exmouth Junction concrete works, the bridge survives to this day, as does that to the east of it, which once allowed passengers to cross between the station platforms, although the latter is no longer in use. With the decline in holiday traffic that resulted from the increase in car ownership during the 1960s, the station was closed with the Seaton branch on 7 March 1966. All the facilities on the Down platform were removed and it is now heavily overgrown, but the original William Tite station building and the skeletal steelwork for the canopy on the opposite side of the line, now in private ownership, are still standing. No. 30832 was withdrawn from Exmouth Junction in January 1964 and was cut up at Eastleigh Works soon afterwards. *Dave Marriot*

**Right:** Ex-LSWR Drummond Class M7 0-4-4T No. 30045 stands at the branch platform at Seaton Junction on 16 May 1959. Developed from the earlier Adams T1 and O2 classes, the M7s were originally intended to be used on suburban services in and out of Waterloo; however, when the first of the tanks entered service in 1897, they were not required for these duties as there was a large number of relatively new tank engines available and they were instead used on semi-fast services. After one was involved in a high-speed derailment near Tavistock in 1898, the locomotives were quickly redeployed onto other duties. The subsequent electrification of the branches to Hampton Court and Shepperton, the Hounslow and Kingston Loops, and the lines to Guildford via Woking, Cobham and Epsom at 600 V DC meant that during the early 20th century the class, which eventually consisted of 105 locomotives, became increasingly used on rural branches, although they continued to appear in Waterloo for a time on stopping services along the main line, on empty coaches stock services to and from Clapham Junction and also on trains to Guildford and Reading. As well as in the West of England, after the formation of the SR in 1923, members of the class could be found as far afield as Kent. Under BR they also found use on the branch lines of East and West Sussex. In the case of No. 30045, which was a push-pull-fitted example, it spent most of its later life at Exmouth Junction, being based there from September 1951 until its withdrawal in December 1962. It was scrapped at Eastleigh Works the following year. *Dave Marriot*

**Below:** But for a short section at 1 in 250, the climb from the former Seaton Junction station to the eastern portal of Honiton Tunnel involves almost five miles of climbing at a gradient of 1 in 80, which would have proved no easy task for the crews of steam locomotives in charge of heavy trains. Bulleid West Country Class 4-6-2 No. 34096 "Trevone" is captured climbing the bank with a lengthy train heading towards Exeter on 16 May 1959. Taking its name from a small seaside village near Padstow, the locomotive was built by BR at Brighton Works in November 1949 and spent the first eight years of its life working on the South Eastern Division of the Southern Region, based at Ramsgate motive power depot. Electrification saw it transferred to Exmouth Junction in December 1957, however, and it remained there until its withdrawal in September 1964, which came only a little over three years after its rebuilding at Eastleigh Works in April 1961. Having travelled a total of 722 328 miles during its 15 years of service, the locomotive was scrapped by the Bird Group at Bynea, Carmarthenshire in March 1965. *Dave Marriot*

**Right:** Ex-SR Maunsell Class N15 4-6-0 No. 30448 "Sir Tristram" leads a short train of Bulleid coaches eastwards away from Sidmouth Junction on 15 May 1959. Named after a contemporary of King Arthur and Knight of the Round Table who spent much of his life on the run after falling hopelessly in love with an Irish princess, Iseult, who was supposed to marry his uncle, King Mark of Cornwall, the locomotive was built at Eastleigh Works in May 1925. Having spent the entirety of its BR career based at Salisbury, it was withdrawn around a year after this photograph was taken, in August 1960, and was scrapped at Eastleigh later that year. *Dave Marriot*

**Above:** Rebuilt Bulleid Merchant Navy Class 4-6-2 No. 35023 "Holland Africa Line" is seen descending Honiton bank with the Up "Atlantic Coast Express" on 16 May 1959. At the time that this photograph was taken the locomotive was only ten years old, it having been built at Eastleigh Works under the auspices of BR in November 1948. Turned out in malachite green, it was named at Southampton Docks on 24 January 1949 by Mr M A Pelt, who was then the Managing Director of Holland Africa Line, in a joint ceremony that also saw No. 35022 named "Holland America Line". The locomotive lost its malachite green livery in March 1952, it being the last of the Merchant Navies to carry this colour. Rather than being painted into BR express blue, it went straight into BR green livery. Having been rebuilt in February 1957, by which point the locomotive had travelled 433 833 miles, it was transferred from Exmouth Junction to Bournemouth in February 1960, then to Weymouth in October 1966 and finally to Nine Elms in March 1967. The locomotive was eventually withdrawn upon the end of Southern Region steam in July 1967, amassing 941 326 miles during its career, and was sold to J Buttigieg of Newport, Monmouthshire, being scrapped in April 1968. *Dave Marriot*

**Left:** Named after a squadron that was reformed a few weeks before the Battle of Britain at RAF Hendon and flew Hurricanes out of RAF Northolt as part of No. 11 Group RAF under the leadership of Sir Keith Park, Bulleid Battle of Britain Class 4-6-2 No. 34072 "257 Squadron" makes light work of the climb of Honiton bank as it heads westwards at Wilmington on 16 May 1959. *Dave Marriot*

**Above:** Ex-SR Bulleid West Country Class 4-6-2 No. 34023 "Blackmore Vale" passes Sidmouth Junction signal box, an LSWR Type 1 structure, with a westbound train on 17 May 1959. The line to Sidmouth can be seen on the right, while Sidmouth Junction station is to the rear of the photographer. It will come as little surprise that the scene has changed dramatically over the intervening years: the signal box and the junction that it controlled are long gone, the branch having closed in 1967, and the main line has been reduced to a single track. The station, meanwhile, was closed with the branch in 1967, but the development of a large housing estate nearby saw it reopened in 1971, since when it has been known as Feniton. Surprisingly, the locomotive is one of the few things in this photograph that survives, it having been purchased for preservation by the Bulleid Society upon its withdrawal in July 1967. It was initially based at the Longmoor Military Railway at Liss in Hampshire but was later moved to the Bluebell Railway, where it was restored to its SR guise as No. 21C123 "Blackmoor Vale". Note the different spelling of the name, which was carried until the locomotive was repainted into BR green in April 1950 after its second General overhaul.
*Dave Marriot*

**Right:** Still in largely the same condition as when it was built in February 1949, BR Bulleid Merchant Navy Class 4-6-2 No. 35029 "Ellerman Lines" is pictured at Exmouth Junction motive power depot on 17 May 1959. The locomotive was rebuilt at Eastleigh Works four months after this photograph was taken, it being one of the last three members of the class to lose its air-smoothed casing and chain-driven valve gear. *Dave Marriot*

**Below:** Rebuilt Bulleid Merchant Navy Class 4-6-2 No. 35013 "Blue Funnel" leads an eastbound express past Exmouth Junction motive power depot, the Southern Region's main depot in the West of England, on 17 May 1959. The third of the Merchant Navies to be built under Order No. 1189, the locomotive was outshopped from Eastleigh Works in February 1945 as No. 21C13 and entered traffic at Nine Elms depot that same month. It was officially named in an event at Waterloo station on 17 April 1945, with the naming being undertaken by Mr L Holt, a senior partner in the shipping company after which it was named. The nameplates carried for the ceremony, which read "Blue Funnel Line", were removed shortly afterwards and replaced by others reading "Blue Funnel Certum Pete Finem", the Latin translating as "hold true to your course". The locomotive lost its original wartime black livery in favour of malachite green in November 1946 and, having been renumbered as No. 35013 in July 1948, was repainted into BR express blue in August 1950 and then into BR green in December 1952. Following its transfer to Exmouth Junction in March 1954, the locomotive was rebuilt under Jarvis in May 1956, it having covered 517 915 miles up to then. Its stay at Exmouth Junction came to an end in September 1964, it then being moved to Bournemouth depot for a little over two years. From October 1966 to March 1967, it was based at Weymouth. Then, for the final four months of its career, it was allocated to Nine Elms, it being withdrawn from there in July 1967 after covering a total of 1 114 658 miles. The locomotive was scrapped by J Buttigieg of Newport, Monmouthshire in October 1967. Exmouth Junction's coaling tower (in the background above the first coach) outlived it by several years. A relic of the steam era, this was planned to have been blown up. When the charges were detonated, however, the structure simply sat down. In the end it had to be broken up using a ball and chain. *Dave Marriot*

**Above:** With an unidentified classmate visible on the depot in the background, BR Bulleid Battle of Britain Class 4-6-2 No. 34075 "264 Squadron" is pictured passing Exmouth Junction with a westbound service on 17 May 1959. Built at Brighton Works under Order No. 3383, the locomotive was one of those that was originally based on the Southern Region's Eastern Division. Initially allocated to Ramsgate motive power depot, it was transferred to Stewarts Lane in July 1948. Following its official naming in February 1949, it was then moved to Dover Marine in September 1950 but returned to Stewarts Lane a month later. After a further stint at the south London shed, it was reallocated to Dover Marine in January 1951 and remained there until being moved back to Ramsgate in May 1952. It was while based at Ramsgate for the second time that the locomotive lost its original malachite green livery in favour of the BR green carried in this photograph (the late crest was a later addition, however). The subsequent electrification of the lines to the Kent coast saw it transferred to Exmouth Junction to work services over the lines of the South Western Division in September 1957. The locomotive spent some seven years operating out of Exmouth Junction, it eventually being withdrawn from service in April 1964 after accumulating a total mileage of 643 241 and was duly placed into storage. Within a couple of months, it was moved to Exeter St Davids depot for further storage. Then, in September 1964, having been sold to a R S Hayes Ltd, it made what was expected to be its final journey. Having run a hot box, however, it was given a short reprieve, spending around three weeks dumped at Bristol Barrow Road before reaching Bridgend towards the start of November 1964. The locomotive was scrapped the following year, by which point Hayes had been taken over by the Bird Group. *Dave Marriot*

**Left:** BR Bulleid Battle of Britain Class No. 34072 "257 Squadron" rests at Exmouth Junction motive power depot on 17 May 1959. Built at Brighton Works under Order No. 3383, the locomotive had entered traffic at Dover Marine almost 11 years earlier, in April 1948, and whilst there it was principally used on the boat trains to and from London, one of its main duties being the "Night Ferry". The brackets between its nameplates and low-set regimental crests indicate that it would have also been used on the prestigious "Golden Arrow". In connection with the Kent Coast Electrification scheme, the locomotive was moved to Exmouth Junction in February 1958 and was then used to work services to places such as Barnstaple, Bude, Ilfracombe, Padstow, Plymouth and Salisbury. It remained at Exmouth Junction until June 1964 and was latterly based at Eastleigh, from where it was withdrawn in October that year after covering a total of 698 843 miles during its 16 years of service. The locomotive was subsequently sold to the infamous Woodham Brothers Ltd of Barry and arrived at the South Wales scrapyard in February 1965. It languished there for some 19 years before being purchased for preservation by the organisation now known as Southern Locomotives Ltd and was moved to the embryonic Swindon & Cricklade Railway for eventual restoration. It was later moved to the former Swindon Works and was returned to steam ahead of the 50th anniversary of the Battle of Britain in September 1990. After touring Britain's heritage railways, it was moved to the Swanage Railway in October 1992 and has been based there ever since. *Dave Marriot*

**Below:** Ex-SR Bulleid West Country Class 4-6-2 No. 34007 "Wadebridge" pauses in between duties at Exmouth Junction on 17 May 1959. *Dave Marriot*

**Above:** Bulleid Battle of Britain Class 4-6-2 No. 34078 "222 Squadron" arrives at Exeter Central on 2 June 1963. One of the first of the locomotives to be built with a 9 ft-wide cab, which precluded its use over the Hastings line, No. 34078 was outshopped from BR's Brighton Works in July 1948 and entered service at Ramsgate motive power depot soon afterwards. It was named in November 1948 after an RAF fighter squadron that took part in one of most dangerous parts of the Battle of Britain, the assault on Fighter Command's inland airfields during the summer of 1940, and was later involved in both the Dunkirk evacuations and also the invasion of north-west Europe before becoming one of the RAF's first fighter jet squadrons in the summer of 1945. Repainted into BR green in August 1951, the locomotive was transferred to Bricklayers Arms in June 1959 and then to Exmouth Junction in January 1961. It was one of only a small number of Bulleid Pacifics that kept its original 5500 gallon tender (No. 3328) until its withdrawal, which came in September 1964. The locomotive covered a total of 779 643 miles during its short life. It was scrapped by the Birds Group at Morriston, Swansea in December 1964. *Dave Marriot*

**Above right:** The same locomotive is seen on an eastbound service at Exeter Central later that same day. Note the two carriages on the adjacent Up Relief Line, which would later be attached to an Up express. These vehicles started life as one of the eight two-car restaurant-buffet sets introduced into service in 1949 as a result of co-operation between the Hotel Executive and Railway Executive. Also designed by Bulleid, these sets consisted of a Kitchen-Buffet car and a Restaurant car. When new, they could be easily identified from their distinctive appearance, with the Kitchen-Buffet cars being partially decorated as half-timbered inns, which led to them being referred to as Tavern cars. Part of their lower panels, which were painted in crimson, were lined out to represent brickwork. The cream panelling above was broken up by black banding and leaded light windows. Each of the vehicles also carried vitreous enamel plates that were specially painted in the style of an inn sign. Their names included "White Horse", "Jolly Tar", "Dolphin", "Three Plovers", "The Bull", "The Salutation", "The Green Man" and "The Crown". Internally, they were similarly styled, with rough-surfaced whitewashed walls and ceiling panels set between dark oak beams, from which period square metal lanterns were hung. They also had dark oak settles, seating up to 12 passengers, and tables placed against the walls. Continuing the theme, which was believed to have been inspired by The Chequers Inn at Pulborough in Sussex, the floor covering mimicked the black and red tiling that could be found in country inns at the time. The only modern features, from the public's point of view at least, were the stainless steel and plastic of the cocktail bar and snack counter. With seating for up to 24 First Class and 46 Third Class passengers, the adjoining Restaurant cars had a similar half-timbered effect. Their appearance was much more modern, however, with polished light-figured oak being used for the timbers and wall frame, buff plastic for the wall panels and concealed fluorescent lighting set in the ceiling in place of the old metal lanterns used in the Tavern car. Opinions of the vehicles were mixed. Although the public seemed to enjoy travelling in them, those in power did not, calling the coaches "Tudoresque monstrosities". Even so, they remained in service for around a decade before being rebuilt as more conventional vehicles with full height windows. *Dave Marriot*

**Below:** With the sidings alongside emphasising the 1-in-37 gradient between Exeter St Davids and Exeter Central stations, Bulleid Battle of Britain Class 4-6-2 No. 34078 "222 Squadron" is seen approaching the Queen Street overbridge at the south-west end of Exeter Central on 2 June 1963. Judging by the previous image, the train appears to be short enough for the locomotive not to have needed assistance; however, many trains had to be helped up the bank, this duty often being undertaken by one of the eight ex-SR Maunsell Z Class 0-8-0Ts, Nos. 30950–30957, which were designed for shunting heavy trains within large marshalling yards such as that at Exmouth Junction. *Dave Marriot*

# CHAPTER 3
## THE SOUTH DEVON MAIN LINE

Having reached Exeter St Davids, we continue to follow the route that was taken by Southern Region services from Waterloo to the various destinations that it served in the north of Devon and Cornwall as far as Cowley Bridge Junction. Situated on the northern outskirts of Exeter, this is where the ex-LSWR line towards Crediton left the former Bristol & Exeter Railway (B&ER) route towards Taunton, over which the LSWR had been granted running powers from Exeter St Davids. This arrangement meant that this part of the line was particularly busy, and it is easy to understand why in later years when the tracks were shared between Bulleid Pacifics and the likes of Collett's "Castles" and "Kings" that it was popular with photographers. After this brief deviation, we return to Exeter St Davids to join the South Devon Main Line to Plymouth, a journey of just over 50 miles.

What is now known as the South Devon Main Line was opened by the South Devon Railway (SDR) in 1846–49, it later being taken over by the GWR to form part of its route from Paddington to Penzance. It was built as a broad gauge line but was converted to standard gauge in May 1892. From Exeter, the line runs alongside the Exe Estuary, passing through Exminster and Starcross before reaching the coast at Dawlish Warren. It then continues along the foot of the red sandstone cliffs at Dawlish on a section of sea wall before turning inland at Teignmouth to run alongside the estuary of the River Teign to Newton Abbot, where services to Paignton leave the main line.

### *Newton Abbot*

The site of the only intermediate station of significant size on this part of our route, Newton Abbot is also where passengers would have once changed trains for stations along the Moretonhampstead branch or the connecting Teign Valley line, passenger services over which were withdrawn in the late 1950s. As the former base of the SDR, it was for many years also the site of a locomotive, carriage and wagon works, which was situated on the east side of the station, along with a motive power depot featuring an eight-road engine shed built by the GWR in the 1890s. The depot was extensively rebuilt in the 1960s to accommodate the Western Region's new diesel-hydraulic locomotives but became redundant in the decades that followed and has since been demolished.

### *Brunel's atmospheric railway*

Leaving Newton Abbot behind, we take a brief look at the Brixham branch (closed 1963) before continuing westwards towards Totnes and on to Plymouth. In contrast with the earlier coastal section, the gradients to the west of Newton Abbot are particularly difficult; the westbound climb to Dainton summit involves around two miles at gradients of up to 1 in 36, and not much further on from that trains are faced with four and a quarter miles at gradients of up to 1 in 45 on the climb to the summit of Rattery bank, making this one of the most difficult sections of main line railway in Britain.

When he set out the route of the SDR, Isambard Kingdom Brunel planned to overcome the gradients that were encountered by using an atmospheric system, which he had seen demonstrated on the Kingston & Dalkley Railway in Ireland. This system was successfully implemented between Exeter and Newton Abbot, though, it was not without its problems. The leather flaps that were used to seal the top of the slotted tubes froze solid in winter, while in summer they dried out and cracked, which prevented the flaps from working properly, causing not only disruption to services but also significant increases in costs as the pumping stations worked to overcome the resulting leaks. With attempts to treat the leather having failed and its manufacturer refusing to replace it, Brunel eventually had to concede that the system would have to be abandoned and the line worked by traditional steam locomotives, which meant that most trains either had to be double-headed or required the assistance of a banking engine when travelling between Newton Abbot and Plymouth. These practices were done away with upon the introduction of diesel traction; however, loads still have to be limited in some cases.

Although the atmospheric system failed to progress beyond Newton Abbot, work was started on the construction of at least some of the engine houses, one of which still stands alongside the station at Totnes, where the former Ashburton branch joined the main line. Never used for its intended purpose, this was purchased by a diary during the 1930s and incorporated into its milk processing plant. The building was granted a Grade II listing in 2008 in recognition of its historic interest.

### *The Lee Moor Tramway*

Having skirted the southern edge of Dartmoor for around ten miles, the line encounters another severe gradient as we near the end of this part of our journey at Plymouth, this being the 1 in 42 Hemerdon bank. Then, after passing the freight yard at Tavistock Junction, which was until 1962 where trains towards Launceston via Tavistock turned to the north, it follows the River Plym for a short distance before reaching the junction at the eastern end of the triangle formed by the stub of the former Sutton Harbour branch, the curve that was once used by SR services heading to and from Plymouth Friary and the South Devon Main Line, in the centre of which was where Laira motive power depot used to be located. This junction also marks the point where the Lee Moor Tramway was crossed.

A privately owned mineral railway that was built in the mid-1800s to carry china clay from the southern slopes of Dartmoor to the quays at Plymouth, the Lee Moor Tramway was unusual in being built to a gauge of 4 ft 6 in, which was termed Dartmoor gauge. Apart from two gravity-worked inclines, where trains of loaded wagons were used to balance the empties that were returning uphill, the tramway was operated solely by horses until 1899. Increasing volumes of traffic led to two Peckett 0-4-0STs being acquired that year to work the section between the inclines, but as time went on these too were replaced, with pipelines eventually being installed to allow the china clay to be moved in slurry form. By the late 1940s, most of the tramway was disused. The section between Marsh Mills and Maddock's concrete plant at Laira remained open until 1960, however, with occasional trains of sand running over this to maintain the right of way over the South Devon Main Line. The flat crossing was last used on 26 August 1960, after which the tramway was dismantled.

# THE SOUTH DEVON MAIN LINE AND ITS CONNECTIONS

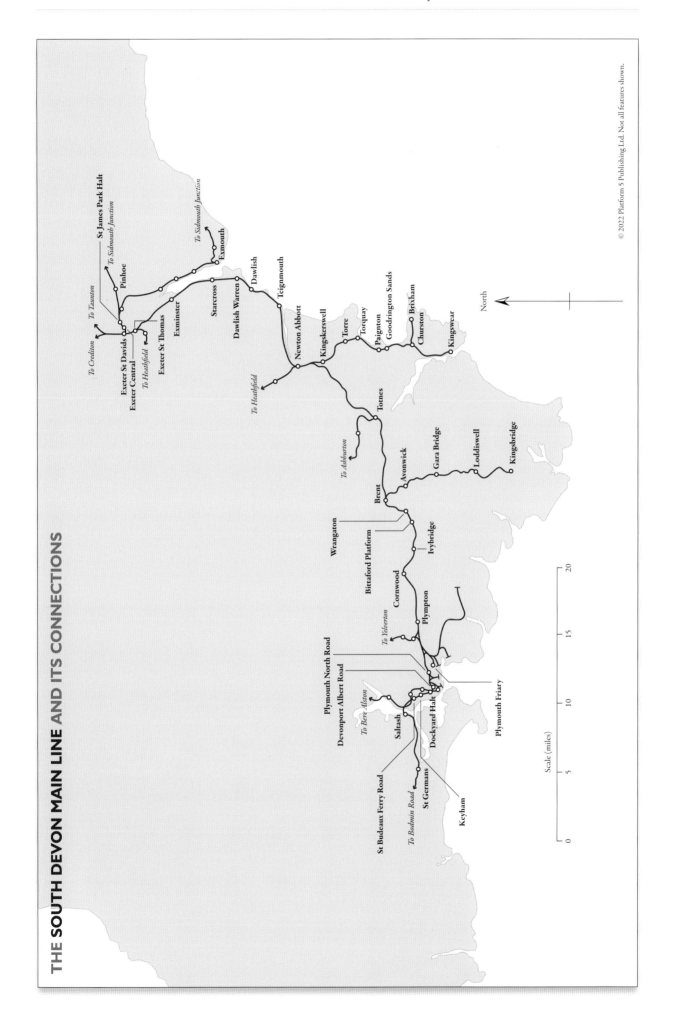

North

Scale (miles)
0    5    10    15    20

To Taunton
To Sidmouth Junction
St James Park Halt
Pinhoe
To Credinn
Exmouth
Exeter St Davids
To Heathfield
Exeter Central
Exeter St Thomas
Exminster
Starcross
Dawlish
Dawlish Warren
Teignmouth
Newton Abbot
To Heathfield
Kingskerswell
Torre
Torquay
Paignton
Goodrington Sands
Brixham
Churston
Kingswear
Totnes
To Ashburton
Avonwick
Gara Bridge
Loddiswell
Kingsbridge
Brent
Wrangaton
Bittaford Platform
Ivybridge
Cornwood
To Yelverton
Plympton
Plymouth North Road
Devonport Albert Road
To Bere Alston
Plymouth Friary
Saltash
Dockyard Halt
St Budeaux Ferry Road
St Germans
To Bodmin Road
Keyham

© 2022 Platform 5 Publishing Ltd. Not all features shown.

**Above:** Seen shortly after passing Cowley Bridge, rebuilt Bulleid Battle of Britain Class 4-6-2 No. 34062 "17 Squadron" approaches Exeter on 14 June 1961 with a train to Waterloo. Built at Brighton Works, the locomotive had entered service just over 14 years earlier in May 1947 as No. 21C162, painted malachite green. It was initially allocated to Ramsgate motive power depot. Having been repainted into BR green, it was renumbered as No. 34062 and gained its name (without ceremony) during January 1949. The locomotive was transferred to Nine Elms in March the following year and remained there until June 1951, after which it was based at Exmouth Junction. It was rebuilt into the condition seen here at Eastleigh Works after 543 488 miles and re-entered service in March 1959, but only saw a further five years' service, its withdrawal coming in June 1964. It travelled a total of 836 579 miles during its 17 years of operation and was scrapped by the Bird Group at Bridgend sometime between June 1965 and June 1966. *Dave Marriot*

**Above:** Ex-SR Bulleid Battle of Britain Class 4-6-2 No. 34066 "Spitfire" leads a train to Waterloo into Exeter on 14 June 1961. Another product of Brighton Works, the locomotive entered traffic towards the start of September 1947 as No. 21C166. It was the second of the locomotives to be built with a wedge-shaped cab and three side windows. When new, Nos. 21C101–21C164 were equipped with cabs that had only two side windows and narrow lookouts at the front, which restricted the view of the road ahead. The positioning of the vacuum ejector controls made this even more of a problem on the driver's side. As such, the cab design was revised, the wedge shape allowing the size of the front windows to be increased but meaning that there was less space for those on the sides. No. 21C165 onwards were built with these new cabs, while the earlier locos had theirs changed as they were overhauled.

One of only two Battle of Britains to be named after aircraft, its naming took place in a ceremony at the former London terminus of the LSWR on 16 September 1947, this being carried out by Sir Hew Kilney, Managing Director of Vickers-Armstrongs (Aircraft) Ltd, which produced the famous fighter planes. Renumbered as No. 34066 by BR in February 1949, the locomotive was repainted into BR green in May the following year, by which time it had been transferred from Ramsgate to Stewarts Lane. Whilst allocated to the south London depot, on the evening of 4 December 1957 it was involved in an incident on the South Eastern Main Line at Lewisham, which resulted in the deaths of 90 people and serious injuries to more than 100 others. Having passed a signal at danger in heavy fog, the locomotive, which was working the 16.56 from Cannon Street to Ramsgate, collided with the rear of the 17.18 from Charing Cross to Hayes at approximately 30 mph. The two rearmost vehicles of the Hayes service suffered moderate damage, but the third from the back was telescoped. Not only this, the impact of the collision caused the locomotive's tender and the leading coach of its train to derail, which caused an overbridge carrying the North Kent Line to be demolished and two coaches to be crushed. It is to this date the third-worst railway accident in the UK.

After re-entering service, the locomotive was transferred to Exmouth Junction in January 1961. It remained there until August 1964 and was withdrawn from Salisbury shed in September 1966 with a recorded mileage of 652 908. It was scrapped by J Buttigieg of Newport, Monmouthshire in January 1967. *Dave Marriot*

**Left:** Ex-LSWR Drummond 700 Class 0-6-0 No. 30691 heads a mixed freight into Exeter on 16 June 1961. Built by Dübs & Co in March 1897, the locomotive, which had been allocated to Exmouth Junction motive power depot since November 1954, was withdrawn within a matter of weeks of this photograph being taken. It was scrapped at Eastleigh Works in September 1961. *Dave Marriot*

**Right:** Bulleid Battle of Britain Class 4-6-2 No. 34081 "92 Squadron" passes Cowley Bridge on 16 June 1961 with a service from Ilfracombe to Exeter Central. Built at Ashford Works, the locomotive entered service at Ramsgate in September 1948 wearing malachite green livery and British Railways lettering on the tender. It was repainted into BR green at Brighton Works in April 1950 and upon the completion of this its nameplates were fitted for the first time, the locomotive being named after a Spitfire squadron that was based at Biggin Hill during the Battle of Britain. It continued to operate on the former Eastern Section of the SR until September 1957, when the completion of the Kent Coast Electrification scheme rendered it and many of its classmates redundant, after which it was based at Exmouth Junction. Upon the Western Region's takeover of Exmouth Junction in June 1964 the locomotive would be transferred to Eastleigh, but its withdrawal came just two months later. It covered a total of 741 511 miles during its 16 years' service. Having been sold to Woodham Brothers Ltd, it was hauled from Eastleigh to Barry on 2 April 1965 in convoy with Nos. 34058, 34067 and 34073 by No. 34006. Ironically, all except No. 34006 were saved for preservation, No. 34081 being purchased by the Battle of Britain Locomotive Preservation Society in September 1973. It eventually left the South Wales scrapyard in November 1976, it becoming the 86th locomotive to do so, and was moved initially to British Sugar's Peterborough site. Later moved to the nearby Nene Valley Railway, in March 1998 it moved for the first time under its own power in 34 years and at the time of publication the locomotive is enjoying its second period of operation in preservation. *Dave Marriot*

**Below:** Ex-GWR Collett Castle Class 4-6-0 No. 7001 "Sir James Milne" is pictured near Cowley Bridge while working a westbound express on 14 June 1961.

Developed from Churchward's "Star" Class, which introduced the template of a four-cylinder 4-6-0 with long-travel valves and a Belpaire firebox that was followed by all the GWR's subsequent express passenger locomotive designs, the "Castles" were designed to meet the need for more powerful locomotives to replace the "Stars" on the GWR's heaviest express trains. The first of the class, No. 4073 "Caerphilly Castle", was outshopped from Swindon Works in August 1923, with a further nine examples having been built by the end of April 1924. Such was the success of the design that the class eventually totalled 171 members, including 16 locomotives that were rebuilt from those belonging to other classes – mostly "Stars", with production continuing until August 1950. Although various changes were made to the design over time, no other class of express passenger steam locomotive was built over such a long period in the history of Britain's railways.

No. 7001 was built as part of Lot No. 357 during 1946, it being released from Swindon Works in April of that year and allocated from new to Cardiff Canton motive power depot. A transfer to Old Oak Common, its base at the time of this photograph being taken, took place in January 1948, with the locomotive being renamed "Sir James Milne" the following month to commemorate the passing of the GWR (Milne was the General Manager of the GWR from 1929 to 1947). The locomotive was originally named "Denbigh Castle", it being the third member of the class to carry this name after No. 5049, which was renamed "Earl of Plymouth" in August 1937 and No. 5074, which was renamed "Hampden" in January 1941. The name eventually reappeared on No. 7032 in June 1950.

Having been fitted with a double chimney and four-row superheater whilst at Swindon Works for a Heavy General overhaul during the summer of 1960, No. 7001 was transferred from Old Oak Common to Wolverhampton's Stafford Road shed in August 1961. Its withdrawal from service came shortly after it was reallocated to Oxley in September 1963, with its scrapping being undertaken by George Cohen, Sons & Co Ltd of Morriston, Swansea during April 1964. *Dave Marriot*

**Below:** Ex-SR Maunsell N Class 2-6-0 No. 31838 approaches Cowley Bridge Junction on 16 June 1961 with a train towards Wadebridge via Lydford. No. A838, as it was numbered when built in 1924, was one of the second batch of the class, which were assembled at Ashford Works using parts produced at the Royal Arsenal, Woolwich as part of a scheme to find work for the skilled labour there after the end of the Great War (World War I). Following trials of No. A815 and No. A825 on the Waterloo–Guildford route, most of the Woolwich Arsenal locos were allocated to the SR's Western Section and these were often used to work trains over the steeply graded lines to the west of Exeter. Based at Exmouth Junction throughout its BR career, No. 31838 would be one of 22 N Class Moguls remaining there at the beginning of 1964. In February of that year, it became the first of these to be withdrawn, however. All except No. 31842, which was transferred to Guildford, were similarly withdrawn by September 1964. No. 31838 was one of only two of these that would go to Eastleigh Works to be dismantled. The rest were sold to the South Wales scrapyards. *Dave Marriot*

**Above:** With what we can ascertain from its headcode discs is one of the first 12 D 800 series "Warship" (Class 42) diesel hydraulics alongside, Collett Castle Class 4-6-0 No. 5020 "Trematon Castle" stands on an express at Exeter St Davids on 15 June 1961. The locomotive, which was built at the GWR's Swindon Works in July 1932, was allocated to Exeter from June 1960 to September 1961. It was subsequently transferred to Cardiff Canton, where it spent much of its early BR years, and then in June 1962 to Llanelly, from where it was withdrawn a matter of months later. Details of its scrapping are unknown. The building after which the locomotive was named is located near Saltash, overlooking Plymouth Sound. It was built in 1068 by Robert, Count of Mortain and the second Earl of Cornwall, to strengthen the hold of William the Conqueror after the Battle of Hastings. The Norman walls remain standing, although in ruins, while the castle keep, which dates from the 12th century, and a later gatehouse are both in good condition. The castle has never been used for its original purpose, although it was used for a time to store the looted gold, silver and emeralds that Sir Francis Drake brought back from his round-the-world voyage in 1580.
*Dave Marriot*

**Left:** Ex-GWR Collett 1400 Class 0-4-2T No. 1468 ambles across Red Cow crossing at the north end of Exeter St Davids on 26 September 1959. The locomotive, which was built at Swindon in February 1936 and entered service as No. 4868, was withdrawn from Oxford shed less than three years after this photo was taken, in March 1962. It was disposed of in March 1965 by John Cashmore Ltd of Newport, Monmouthshire.
*Dave Marriot*

**Below:** A stark contrast from its classmate being polished on the left of shot, heavily weathered Collett 4073 Class 4-6-0 No. 4079 "Pendennis Castle" hauls a mixed freight through Exeter St Davids on 14 June 1961. The seventh of the 171 "Castles" to come off the production line at Swindon, the locomotive was outshopped in February 1924. Named after a fort near Falmouth, it shot to fame in 1925 when it was lent to the LNER to be compared with the new Gresley Class A1 4-6-2s. Working heavy trains over the southern end of the East Coast Main Line between King's Cross and Doncaster, the locomotive outperformed the larger Pacifics in every way, regularly completing the climb to Finsbury Park in less than six minutes (a time that the Pacifics were unable to match) and being more economical in terms of coal and water consumption. Prior to returning to the GWR, between May and October 1925 it was displayed alongside No. 4472 "Flying Scotsman" at the second British Empire Exhibition at Wembley, with a sign proclaiming it to be the most powerful express passenger locomotive in the country. Once back at Old Oak Common, the locomotive re-entered normal service, being used to work trains to destinations in South Wales and the West Country. It was later based at various sheds across the Western Region, including Hereford, Gloucester, Stafford Road, Bristol Bath Road, Taunton, St Philip's Marsh and Swindon, and was eventually withdrawn from service at St Philip's Marsh in May 1964.

Shortly before its withdrawal, on 9 May 1964 the locomotive was involved in a Paddington–Plymouth railtour commemorating the 60th anniversary of GWR Churchward 3700 Class 4-4-0 No. 3440 "City of Truro" becoming the first steam locomotive to (allegedly) achieve a speed of 100 mph, on the descent of Whiteball bank at Wellington in Somerset. Titled "The Great Western High Speed Railtour", but more commonly known by its headcode – 1Z48, this was to be the swansong of Great Western steam. It would be the last chance for any high-speed running behind steam on the Western Region (permission had been given to attempt to hit 100 mph on the return journey, which was via Bristol and Badminton, between Hullavington and Little Somerford) and as such nothing was left to chance. Prior to the tour's operation, the condition of the remaining "Castles" was reviewed, with the four best examples being chosen to haul the trip. No. 4079 was one of those selected. It and its three classmates were given boiler washouts, their tender tanks were cleaned out and they were coaled using Ogilvie washed coal, which was believed to be the best Welsh coal available at the time. This, unfortunately, may have hindered the locomotive more than it helped. Each locomotive was given two firemen. It is believed that the high rate of firing combined with the high-quality, hot-burning coal caused the locomotive's firebars to melt as its speed exceeded 90 mph, leading to its failure and consequent replacement at Westbury by Hawksworth 6959 Class 4-6-0 No. 6999 "Capel Dewi Hall". Standby locos had been positioned at key points along the train's route, but the nearest "Castle" was in Taunton, No. 7025 "Sudeley Castle" taking over from there. The train was returned from Plymouth by No. 7029 "Clun Castle", which worked it as far as Bristol Temple Meads, and No. 5054 "Earl of Ducie", which took it forward from Bristol to Paddington.

After its withdrawal, the locomotive passed into preservation. It was initially based at Didcot, then, after another change of hands, at Market Overton in Rutland, later moving to Steamtown at Carnforth. Gauging problems meant that there was little opportunity for it to run in the North of England, however, and so in 1977 it was sold to Hamersley Iron, one of Australia's largest producers of iron ore, for use on excursion trains over the firm's private railway across the Pilbara region of Western Australia. In 1989, during the country's bicentennial celebrations, it was reunited with its old rival "Flying Scotsman" at Perth, but increased freight traffic on the Hamersley Railway and other operational difficulties meant that it saw little use after this and its final steaming in the southern hemisphere took place in October 1994. With uncertainties over its future, the locomotive was subsequently gifted to the Great Western Society and has since been repatriated to the UK, it arriving at Avonmouth Docks on 8 July 2000 after a ten-week voyage via the Pacific Rim, the Panama Canal, the Eastern Seaboard of the USA and then across the Atlantic Ocean. This made it the only 4-6-0 to have circumnavigated the globe and the second steam locomotive to do so after "Flying Scotsman". *Dave Marriot*

▌ **Above:** Collett 6000 Class 4-6-0 No. 6024 "King Edward I" passes Exminster with the outward leg of Past Time Rail's "Devonian" railtour, 1Z24 07.00 Ealing Broadway–Plymouth, on 13 November 2004. *Rhys Jones*

**Left:** With an unidentified "Castle" in the background, ex-GWR Collett 7200 Class 2-6-2T No. 7224 passes Exeter St Davids with a train of unfitted mineral wagons on 15 June 1961. Rebuilt from Churchward 4200 Class and Collett 5205 Class 2-8-0Ts, which were designed to work coal trains in and around the Welsh valleys, the 7200s were unique in being Britain's only 2-8-2Ts. They were also the largest tank engines to run on the former GWR system. Their development was prompted by the stock market crash of 1929, which caused a considerable drop in coal traffic, making many of the aforementioned 2-8-0Ts redundant. To make them more useful, Collett took the decision to rebuild the locomotives with a greater coal carrying capacity, giving them an improved range. This entailed their frames being extended by 4 ft and the addition of a trailing wheelset. Rebuilt from No. 5259, No. 7224 was part of the second batch of locomotives, which were outshopped from Swindon Works between August 1935 and February 1936. It entered traffic in November 1935 and spent much of its life in South Wales, but at the time of this photograph being taken it was based at Exeter. It was the only one of the 54-strong class to be allocated to the adjacent motive power depot. Its stay was only a short one, however, and in November 1961, only five months after it had arrived, it was transferred to Ebbw Junction, from where it was withdrawn in November 1962. The locomotive was cut up by R S Hayes Ltd at Tremains Yard, Bridgend in January 1964. *Dave Marriot*

**Below:** Double-chimnied Collett 4073 Class 4-6-0 No. 5057 "Earl Waldegrave" approaches Dawlish Warren on 18 September 1959 with what is believed to be the 11.10 Swansea–Penzance service. Built at the GWR's Swindon Works during June 1936, the locomotive was originally named "Penrice Castle" but was later given the name that was destined to be carried by Collett 3200 Class 4-4-0 No. 3214. The "Dukedogs", as they were known, were chosen to carry the name of Earls with connections to the GWR following repeated requests from aristocratic directors of the company. The locomotives did not find favour with those involved, however. Although they were officially new, they were built using the frames of the redundant Dean 3300 Class "Bulldogs" and the boilers from the worn-out Dean 3252 Class "Dukes", which gave them an old-fashioned appearance. The names were therefore given to some of the new "Castles" (Nos. 5043–5062) instead. No. 5057 was eventually withdrawn from service in March 1964, at which point it was based at Old Oak Common motive power depot in west London. It was scrapped at Swindon Works in August 1964. *Dave Marriot*

**Below:** Ex-GWR Collett 6100 Class 2-6-2T No. 6166, one of 70 locomotives that were built as a higher-powered development of the earlier Collett 5101 Class 2-6-2Ts for work on suburban services around London, brings a stopping service into Dawlish Warren on 18 September 1959. Not long after this the locomotive was reallocated from Newton Abbot to Plymouth's Laira motive power depot. It remained at Laira until its withdrawal in January 1962 and was scrapped at Swindon Works four months later. It covered some 665 152 miles during its 26 years of operation. *Dave Marriot*

**Below:** Ex-GWR Collett 5101 Class 2-6-2T No. 4174 accelerates away from Dawlish on 19 September 1959. It is about to plunge into the 209 yard-long Kennaway Tunnel, which carries the railway beneath Lea Mount and is the first of five tunnels along this part of the route, the others being Coryton, Phillot, Clerk's and Parson's Tunnels. When the route of the railway was planned out it did not include any tunnels hereabouts, however. It was originally to have run along the foot of the cliffs, but the local fishing community was concerned that this would result in Boat, Coryton and Shell Coves being lost, along with much of the beach, so this prompted a change of plans that would see the railway built inside the short sea wall that was constructed in the late 1830s and the cliffs being cut back in places to accommodate this. *Dave Marriot*

**Above:** The first of the 30 Collett 6000 Class 4-6-0s to be built at Swindon Works, No. 6000 "King George V" bursts out of Parson's Tunnel, on the approach to Teignmouth, with a westbound express on 19 September 1959. Despite its unkempt condition, the locomotive was at one time the pride of the GWR fleet.

Built in response to rising passenger numbers and increasing train weights, the "Kings" represented the final development of Churchward's "Stars" and Collett's "Castles". To avoid overloading certain structures, the design of the latter was limited to a maximum axle loading of 20 tons, meaning that the locomotives were unable to haul the heaviest expresses without assistance. A programme of bridge renewals in the years that followed their introduction, coupled with the findings of the Department of Scientific and Industrial Research's Bridge Stress Committee, which gave engineers a better understanding of the impact of hammer blow, meant that the GWR Civil Engineer was able to raise the axle load limit for what were then referred to as the "Super Castles" to 22½ tons. Taking full advantage of this, the new locomotives were fitted with Standard No. 12 boilers, which were enlarged versions of the Standard No. 7 boilers fitted to the Churchward 4700 Class 2-8-0s. This gave them a maximum boiler pressure of 250 psi and a 34.3 sq ft fire grate, the largest of any British narrow firebox locomotive design. By increasing the cylinder stroke from 26 in to 28 in, using 6 ft 6 in diameter wheels rather than the 6 ft 8½ in and boring out the cylinders on the first six locomotives to 16¼ in opposed to 16 in as on the "Castles", this gave the locomotives a tractive effort of 40 300 lbf, which made them the most powerful locomotives in Britain at the time. The SR's "Lord Nelsons" took this title from the "Castles" in 1926 and since then the management of the GWR had been keen for a locomotive design to reclaim it for the company. Operational experience soon showed that the outer cylinders caused clearance problems, however, so these were replaced during the locomotives' first overhauls, resulting in their tractive effort falling to 39 700 lbf.

It was originally planned that the locomotives would be named after notable cathedrals; however, an invitation for a GWR locomotive to be featured in the Baltimore & Ohio Railroad's centenary celebrations in 1927 resulted in the class instead being named after kings, with 6000 being named after the reigning monarch at the time of its construction. It was this locomotive that was despatched to the USA. During the celebrations, it was presented with a brass bell and cabside medallions to commemorate the event. Upon its return from the USA, the locomotive was initially based at Old Oak Common motive power depot in west London. It later had spells at Laira and Bristol Bath Road before being returned to Old Oak Common in September 1952. After covering a total of 1 910 424 miles, it was withdrawn from service in December 1962. Now part of the National Collection, the locomotive continued to grab headlines by becoming the first locomotive, in 1971, to break the ban on steam locomotives operating on the main line imposed by BR after the end of steam in 1968.

Note the "pillbox" to the right of the tunnel portal, which was built as part of a national defence system during the Second World War to protect this part of the coastline from invasion. *Dave Marriot*

**Above:** Taken from roughly the same vantage point as the previous photograph but looking in the opposite direction, ex-GWR Collett 4073 Class 4-6-0 No. 5024 "Carew Castle" heads a train to Paddington along the sea wall at Teignmouth on 26 September 1959. The locomotive, which was built at Swindon Works in April 1934 and named after what was originally a Norman stronghold in Pembrokeshire, was shedded at Newton Abbot at the time of this photograph. Having been based there for 12½ years, it was taken out of traffic in May 1962 and was scrapped by John Cashmore Ltd of Newport, Monmouthshire in December that year. *Dave Marriot*

**Below:** Ex-GWR Collett 6000 Class 4-6-0 No. 6013 "King Henry VIII" leads a westbound express out of Parson's Tunnel, between Dawlish and Teignmouth, on 26 September 1959. According to the train's reporting number, which in this case is displayed using three 20 in boards mounted on a 3 ft-wide frame fitted to the locomotive's smokebox door to help signalmen correctly identify the approaching train from at least a quarter of a mile away in order to direct it the correct way at junctions, this is the Saturdays-only 09.30 Paddington–Newquay service. Stencilled numbers pasted onto small boards, as shown on Page 101, were also used for this purpose. In some cases, reporting numbers were even chalked or whitewashed onto the front of a locomotive, but it is debatable whether chalk was effective. *Dave Marriot*

**Right:** Ex-GWR Hawksworth 6959 Class 4-6-0 No. 6965 "Thirlestaine Hall" passes Parson's Tunnel signal box with a westbound stopping service on 26 September 1959. Built in 1906 to replace an earlier wooden structure, which dated from 1884, the box was closed in 1909. Having been boarded up, it remained out of use until 1934, when it was reinstated in response to the volume of holiday traffic using the line. After a further 30 years of operation, it closed for good in 1964. The locomotive, which had entered service in July 1944 and took its name from a 19th century mansion in Cheltenham, outlived it by a couple of years. Latterly based at Bristol Barrow Road motive power depot, it was withdrawn in October 1965. It was scrapped in March of the following year by John Cashmore Ltd of Newport, Monmouthshire. *Dave Marriot*

**Below:** Collett Castle Class 4-6-0 No. 7014 "Caerhays Castle" rounds the curve onto the sea wall at Teignmouth with an Up express on 26 September 1959. One of the 30 "Castles" built under BR, No. 7014 was outshopped from Swindon Works in July 1948. Featuring double chimneys, revised draughting, reprofiled outside steam pipes and four-row superheaters amongst other refinements that had been introduced over the years, this and the other 70xx series locomotives, the last of which was completed in 1950, represented the ultimate development of a design dating back to 1923 (although with its heritage going even further back to Churchward's 4000 Class "Star" 4-6-0s, which were designed during the mid-1900s) and put in some outstanding performances during their careers. In the case of No. 7014, this was less than 17 years, the locomotive being withdrawn from service in February 1963. During this time its allocations included Bristol Bath Road (July 1948–September 1960, with a month on loan to Old Oak Common in early 1956), Landore (September–October 1960), St Philip's Marsh (October 1960–August 1961), Old Oak Common (August 1961–June 1962), Stafford Road (June 1962–September 1963), Oxley (September 1963–June 1964) and Tyseley (June 1964–February 1965). The locomotive was promptly disposed of by John Cashmore Ltd at Great Bridge during May 1965. Note the oil reservoir for the Davies and Metcalfe valveless mechanical lubricator on the side of smokebox. No. 7014 was one of only five of the class equipped with this feature, which rather spoilt their look. *Dave Marriot*

**Below:** Instantly identifiable by its unique BR express blue livery, which was applied during the preservation era, rebuilt Bulleid Merchant Navy Class 4-6-2 No. 35005 "Canadian Pacific" approaches the Shaldon road bridge at Teignmouth with the 16.32 Kingswear–Birmingham Snow Hill on 9 September 2000. Organised by Vintage Trains, this trip was significant for several reasons. Pathing difficulties meant that the outward journey had to be routed via Bath and Westbury, extending the total length of the journey to around 450 miles, which at the time was believed to be the highest mileage purely steam-hauled trip for over 30 years. As well as this, during the course of the journey, "Canadian Pacific" passed its millionth mile in service. *Rhys Jones*

**Right:** With Tuckers Maltings and the former Torquay Corporation power station in the background, Collett 5101 Class 2-6-2T No. 4179 is seen working an eastbound service at Newton Abbot on 20 September 1959. The locomotive, which entered service in December 1949, was allocated from new to the nearby Newton Abbot motive power depot. Having been transferred away (to Stafford Road shed at Wolverhampton) in April 1961, it was withdrawn from Tyseley in February 1965 and scrapped by George Cohens, Sons & Co Ltd at Kingsbury in October 1965. *Dave Marriot*

**Left:** Ex-GWR Collett 6000 Class 4-6-0 No. 6024 "King Edward I" and ex-GWR Collett 4073 Class 4-6-0 No. 5029 "Nunney Castle" approach Aller Junction, where the line to Torquay, Paignton and Kingswear, used to leave the South Devon Main Line, with a Pathfinder Tours railtour from Worcester Shrub Hill to Par on 23 April 2005. *Rhys Jones*

**Above:** An autotrain, formed of ex-GWR Collett 1400 Class 0-4-2T No. 1470 and Hawksworth Diagram A43 autocoach No. W 241 W, awaits its departure from Brixham on 17 September 1959. Introduced in the early 20th century to eliminate the need for locomotives to run around their trains at the end of a journey, autocoaches (or autotrailers) were a common sight across much of the former GWR network, particularly on branch lines such as this, although they were also used on some suburban services. The trains could consist of as many as four coaches, two each side of the locomotive, typically at this time a 1400 Class or a Hawksworth 5400/6400 Class 0-6-0PT. A number of Collett 4575 Class 2-6-2Ts were also fitted with the appropriate equipment. Generally, if any more than one autocoach was used, the locomotive would be marshalled in the middle of the train. Play in the linkage system that allowed the driver to control the accompanying locomotive's regulator from the cab of an autocoach meant that this was difficult to operate when there were two of the coaches coupled together. As well as these linkages, the vehicles were also fitted with equipment for their drivers to control the train brakes and large mechanical gongs to warn crossing users and track workers of an approaching train. An electrically operated bell system was provided for the driver to communicate with the fireman, who remained on the footplate of the locomotive to maintain the supply of steam – and also control the valve gear settings, and the guard. Note the retractable steps, which were fitted to enable passengers to get on and off the trains at wayside halts with low platforms. *Dave Marriot*

**Above:** Now with a van in tow, the same pairing is seen arriving at Churston, where the Brixham branch connected with the line to Kingswear. Poor passenger numbers, due in part to competition from more convenient motor bus services, led to the branch being closed less than four years later (in May 1963). By then the autotrains had been replaced with more modern DMUs. No. 1470, which was withdrawn from service at Exeter in October 1962 after 23 years of operation, was scrapped by John Cashmore Ltd at Newport, Monmouthshire in October 1963. *Dave Marriot*

**Below:** With the autocoach on the Brixham shuttle visible in the background, ex-GWR Collett 5101 Class 2-6-2T No. 5178 is pictured a little later the same day leaving Churston with a service to Kingswear. Ordered in 1930 as part of the 30 locomotives (Nos. 5160–5189) that comprised Lot 259, No. 5178 was outshopped from Swindon Works in January 1931 and had a service life of just over 29 years, it being withdrawn at Newton Abbot motive power depot in March 1960 and scrapped at Swindon in June that year. *Dave Marriot*

**Above:** With a lengthy train of BR Mark 1s in tow, ex-GWR Collett 4073 Class 4-6-0s Nos. 5051 "Earl Bathurst" and 5029 "Nunney Castle" put on a fine display as they climb the 1-in-37 gradient on the approach to Dainton summit with 1Z72, the 04.22 Birmingham International–Penzance, on 29 May 2004. The pair had taken over the train, which was organised by Pathfinder Tours and titled "The Cornubian", from an EWS Class 67 diesel locomotive at Taunton. Eagle-eyed readers will, however, notice that there are three lines of text on the headboard. It, in fact, reads "The Bryan Dudley Ward Cornubian", this being a tribute to a well-known footplate inspector who had passed away earlier that year.

Interestingly, both locomotives were turned out from Swindon Works in May 1934 and although they had very different careers, they were withdrawn within a matter of months of each other, No. 5051 being retired from service at Llanelly in May 1963, while No. 5029 was withdrawn from traffic at Cardiff East Dock in December 1963. Having been sold to Woodham Brothers Ltd, both made their way to Barry. In fact, No. 5029 was the last steam locomotive to be delivered to the South Wales scrapyard by rail. After languishing in the sea air there for several years, No. 5051 was purchased by a private individual and in February 1970 it was moved to the embryonic Didcot Railway Centre, which remains its home today. No. 5029 was similarly purchased by a private individual but did not leave Barry until May 1976, by which point it was the last "Castle" remaining there. Having been sold to a consortium that included the Great Western Society, it too was restored at Didcot and has since made numerous appearances at work on the main line. *Rhys Jones*

**Right:**  Only a little over nine years old but already more than halfway through its short life, Hawksworth 6959 Class 4-6-0 No. 7916 "Mobberley Hall" climbs the final few yards to the western portal of Dainton Tunnel with a fitted freight on 23 September 1959. The locomotive, which was named after a 17th century country house in Cheshire and was at this point allocated to Newton Abbot motive power depot, remained in service until December 1964. It was scrapped at Swindon Works in February 1965. Note the sighting mirror above the third vehicle, which enabled the staff of Dainton Sidings signal box to check that eastbound trains were complete as they entered the tunnel (in case the view of their tail lamp was obscured by a passing westbound train). *Dave Marriot*

**Below:**  Heavily weathered ex-GWR Hawksworth 1000 Class 4-6-0 "County of Middlesex" leads a westbound express through the cutting on the approach to the eastern portal of Dainton Tunnel on 23 September 1959. The first of a class of 30, the locomotive was built at the Swindon Works as part of Lot No. 354 in August 1945. Although its outshopping brought a welcome return of lined green locomotives to the GWR network, it caused quite a stir as the locomotive's design, which represented the final development of the Churchward 2900 Class 4-6-0s, included several significant differences to its predecessors, such as a double chimney, one-piece splashers and a flat-sided tender. For many years it was, in fact, the only member of the class to carry a double chimney; however, in an effort to overcome their poor performance, each of its classmates was similarly equipped between 1956 and 1959. Their boiler pressure was reduced from 280 psi to 250 psi around the same time to reduce hammer blow. Initially allocated to Old Oak Common motive power depot in west London, the locomotive was at this point based at Bristol Bath Road. It was withdrawn from service at Swindon in July 1964 and was scrapped by John Cashmore Ltd of Newport, Monmouthshire during the December of that year. *Dave Marriot*

**Below:** Looking to be in considerably better condition than when we last saw it, ex-GWR Collett 6000 Class 4-6-0 No. 6000 "King George V" climbs towards Dainton summit on 23 September 1959 with what is thought to be an Up "Ocean Liner" express from Plymouth to Paddington. This includes two of the eight Collett "Super Saloons", which were built in 1931–32 following a short-lived experiment where Pullman Car Company stock was used on the "Ocean Liners" and also, during its only summer of operation, the "Torquay Pullman". The hire of the Pullmans and their attendants was deemed to be too costly, so the GWR set about building a rake of its own luxury vehicles, which were allotted Nos. 9111–9118. All were originally named after members of the British Royal family, but their names were lost in 1951 when the vehicles were repainted into BR carmine and cream livery. By the late 1950s, the Plymouth boat train market was in decline, with transatlantic travel being dominated by the airlines, so BR withdrew the "Ocean Liner" trains and the "Super Saloons" were redeployed. Being 9 ft 7 in wide over the waist panels, the vehicles, which had to be bow ended to avoid the door handles being out of gauge, were restricted to lines that were originally built as broad gauge. As well as being hired to private parties, for a time they were used on race day specials between Paddington and Newbury Racecourse, but by 1966 all had been withdrawn. *Dave Marriot*

**Above:** Ex-GWR Collett 4900 Class 4-6-0 No. 4936 "Kinlet Hall" and ex-GWR Churchward 4073 Class No. 4098 "Kidwelly Castle" run downgrade towards Totnes at Tigley on 22 September 1959. Although it is evidently not needed at this point in the journey, the presence of the second locomotive between Plymouth and Newton Abbott would have been much appreciated on the difficult climbs to the summits of Hemerdon and Dainton banks. *Dave Marriot*

**Below:** Collett 4900 Class 4-6-0 No. 6933 "Birtles Hall" has steam to spare as it leads Collett 6000 Class 4-6-0 No. 6022 "King Edward III" westwards past Tigley on 22 September 1959. Named after a Cheshire country house, No. 6933 was a Laira locomotive at this time, although it was transferred to Landore shed not long after this (in November 1959). A little over five years later it would be withdrawn, its almost 23-year career coming to an end at Oxley in November 1964. It was subsequently scrapped by John Cashmore Ltd at Great Bridge. No. 6022, meanwhile, which was named after the monarch who reigned as King of England and Lord of Ireland from 1327 until his death in 1377, was allocated at this point to Stafford Road (Wolverhampton). It continued to be based at the West Midlands shed until, after just over 32 years' service, it was withdrawn in September 1962 having completed 1 733 189 miles. The locomotive was scrapped by Cox & Danks Ltd, Langley Green, Oldbury the following year. It was one of 11 "Kings" to be disposed of at the site. *Dave Marriot*

**Above:** Collett 2884 Class 2-8-0 No. 3862 climbs past Tigley towards the summit of Rattery bank with a Class E freight – an express freight, livestock, perishable or ballast train with no less than four vacuum-braked vehicles piped to the engine, or an express freight of limited load not fitted with continuous brakes – on 22 September 1959. Built as a development of the earlier Churchward 2800 Class locos, which were the GWR's first 2-8-0s and indeed the first locomotives of this wheel arrangement to run anywhere in Britain, the 2884s were designed to move heavy freight trains consisting of up to 100 wagons at speeds of 20–30 mph over long distances. Such was the success of the design that the locomotives were used almost all over the GWR network (their axle loading precluded their use on a lot of branch lines) and there were hopes that their construction would continue after Nationalisation; however, the need for further heavy freight locos was fulfilled by Riddles' Standard Class 9F 2-10-0s. No. 3862 was built as one of what became the final batch, being outshopped from Swindon Works in November 1942. It was initially allocated to Oxford, remaining there until October 1947, after which it had a six-year stay at Pontypool Road. From December 1953 to July 1962, it was then based at Laira, spending much of its time either hauling freights such as this over the Devon banks or into Cornwall. From Plymouth it was transferred to Cardiff Canton, but after just a month there it was moved on to Cardiff East Dock, where it remained until September 1963, eventually being withdrawn from service at Croes Newydd in February 1965. It was subsequently sold to Woodham Brothers Ltd of Barry for disposal, arriving at the South Wales scrapyard in July 1965; however, it 1987 it was sold to the LNWR Preservation Society for restoration. *Dave Marriot*

**Below:** With the plume of steam at the rear of the train indicating the presence of a banker, ex-GWR Collett 5101 Class 2-6-2T No. 5174 heads an express freight westward up Rattery bank on 26 September 1959. Allocated at this point to Exeter motive power depot, the locomotive was built at Swindon Works in December 1930 and was withdrawn from service at Birmingham's Tyseley depot in November 1961. Having sustained collision damage to its bunker, it was scrapped at Swindon towards the end of January 1962. *Dave Marriot*

**Right:** Ex-GWR Hawksworth 1000 Class 4-6-0 No. 1007 "County of Brecknock" leads BR Warship Class No. D 806 "Cambrian" and a lengthy train of chocolate and cream-liveried BR Mark 1 coaches eastwards towards Totnes on 22 September 1959. Both built at Swindon Works, the two very different locomotives were separated by less than 14 years, the "County" being outshopped in December 1945 and the "Warship" in June 1959. Surprisingly, it was the former that had the longer life, it eventually being withdrawn in October 1962 after almost 17 years' service and was scrapped during the November of the following year. Though they were much more successful than some of the other classes that were ordered to replace the Western Region's steam locomotive fleet, the "Warships" were withdrawn during the late 1960s and early 1970s after diesel-hydraulics were declared to be non-standard by BR and an instruction was issued for them to be replaced as soon as possible. No. D 806's withdrawal came in November 1972, giving it an active life of almost 13½ years, during which time it covered an impressive 1 281 000 miles. It was scrapped at Swindon Works in May 1975. *Dave Marriot*

**Below:** Ex-GWR Collett 4900 Class 4-6-0 No. 4975 "Umberslade Hall" and ex-GWR Collett 6000 Class 4-6-0 No. 6003 "King George IV" slog towards the summit of Rattery on 24 September 1959. No. 4975 was a local locomotive at this time, being based at Newton Abbott, while No. 6003 was allocated to Old Oak Common. Both were withdrawn within four years of this photograph being taken, No. 4975 coming out of service at Oxford in September 1963 having outlasted the "King" by about 15 months. No. 6003 was withdrawn from service at Cardiff Canton in June 1962 and scrapped at Swindon Works, where it had been built almost 35 years earlier (in September 1962). The "Hall" was eventually disposed of by John Cashmore Ltd of Newport, Monmouthshire in July 1964. *Dave Marriot*

**Below:** GWR Collett 6000 Class 4-6-0 No. 6002 "King William IV" blows off as it heads the 11.00 Penzance–Paddington express, which it would have taken over at Plymouth, towards Totnes on 24 September 1959. Named after the third son of George III who ruled Great Britain and Ireland between June 1830 and June 1837, the locomotive was outshopped from Swindon Works in July 1927 and was based from new at Plymouth's Laira motive power depot. It later spent time working out of Wolverhampton's Stafford Road shed and also at Old Oak Common but was once again based at Laira at the time that this photograph was taken. Having covered 1 891 952 miles in service, it was eventually withdrawn with the introduction of the new timetable in September 1962, which saw the "Kings" that were used on the expresses between Paddington, Birmingham Snow Hill and Birkenhead replaced by diesel traction. Along with ten of its classmates, it was sold to Cox & Danks Ltd and was scrapped at the company's Oldbury site during 1963. *Dave Marriot*

**Above:** An unidentified ex-GWR Churchward 4500 Class 2-6-2T is pictured at Brent on 21 September 1959. As is indicated by the sizeable running in board, this was where passengers changed between services on the main line and those on the Kingsbridge branch, although there were through trains to and from Paddington at weekends. The station, which was situated on the southern edge of Dartmoor, at 229 miles and 54 chains from Paddington, also served the small community of South Brent. Indeed, this was its original purpose, the station's opening coming some 45 years before that of the branch. Passengers for Kingsbridge were expected to use the nearby Wrangaton station, which was named Kingsbridge Road between 1849 and 1895. The people of Kingsbridge and its surrounding districts were unhappy about this, however, and the idea of rail link to the town was put forward as early as 1854. Intended to connect Kingsbridge with Churston on the Dartmouth & Torbay Railway's branch to Kingswear, this met with a positive response from the public, but in truth it was overly ambitious and failed to attract the necessary investment for it to proceed. After ten years had passed, an alternative route for the railway was proposed. This involved a branch being built off the SDR's main line to Plymouth to provide a connection to not only Kingsbridge but also Salcombe on the south Devon coast. Costed at £130 000, this more modest scheme gained enough support to get it as far as Parliament, which authorised the Act for the Kingsbridge & Salcombe Railway on 29 July 1864, but after this things slowed significantly. Deviations from the planned route of the railway meant that more money was needed and although construction work was started, little was done; by 1871 it was proposed that the scheme should be abandoned. Another ten years went by before the idea resurfaced. Once again, there was an enthusiastic reception, but little finance was forthcoming and it was only when the GWR was persuaded to take on the unbuilt line in 1888 that any real progress was made, the line being opened as far as Kingsbridge five years later. The plan for it to continue through to Salcombe was never implemented. Throughout its existence the line relied heavily on leisure traffic, which dwindled considerably as car ownership increased through the 1950s, causing heavy losses and leading to its proposed closure by the infamous Doctor Beeching. Interestingly, this prompted an increase in ridership, but it wasn't enough to save the line. Its closure eventually came in September 1963. It was, however, granted a brief stay of execution beyond the end of that year's summer timetable as the changes to the Western National bus services that would replace the trains did not come into effect until the start of their winter timetable on 16 September 1963. Despite an attempt to reopen the railway as a heritage line, the track was lifted by May 1964. Although its goods facilities were closed on 6 April 1964, the station at Brent remained open for passengers until 5 October 1964. It has since been demolished. *Dave Marriot*

**Right:** A development of the earlier Churchward 4500 Class locomotives featuring larger side tanks and increased water capacity, ex-GWR Collett 4575 Class 2-6-2T No. 5558 stands at Kingsbridge on 18 September 1959. The locomotive, which was built at Swindon in November 1928, was withdrawn from Newton Abbot a little over a year later (in October 1960). It was scrapped at Swindon Works in January 1961. Following the line's closure, the station site was redeveloped as an industrial estate. The main station building survived until 2009, but nowadays the only indicators of the site's former use are a small part of the station platform and the goods shed. *Dave Marriot*

**Above:** Viewed from the opposite end of the station, ex-GWR Collett 6000 Class 4-6-0 No. 6002 "King William IV" is seen passing through Brent with the Up "Royal Duchy", the 11.00 Penzance–Paddington, on 21 September 1959. Note the headboard, which carries the arms of the Duchy of Cornwall. Prior to the service's introduction in January 1957, Royal approval had to be sought before this could be used. Along with many others, the train's title was dropped in June 1965, although it was later reinstated. *Dave Marriot*

# CHAPTER 4
## THE CORNISH MAIN LINE

### *Plymouth*

The final leg of our journey starts at the former Plymouth North Road, which was opened in 1877 to provide a facility that could be run jointly by the GWR and LSWR. It will come as little surprise to readers that the station has changed considerably over the intervening years. During the late 1930s, work was started on a major rebuild, which was intended to increase its capacity so that the nearby Plymouth Millbay and Mutley stations could be closed. The outbreak of World War II delayed the project, but Mutley was closed in July 1939, while air raids caused the premature closure of Plymouth Millbay in 1941. Further reconstruction work took place in the late 1950s. These works were closely linked with the rebuilding of the city centre and saw an eight-storey office block built on the station front, the ground floor of which was used to house the station's booking and enquiry offices, left luggage facilities and a parcels depot. The rebuilt station and tower block were officially opened in March 1962. Meanwhile, the semaphore signalling in the station area was replaced with colour lights in November 1960, with the new Plymouth power signal box being opened at the same time. As such, apart from further changes to its layout in the mid-1970s, the station remains remarkably unchanged from how it was during the latter years of steam in the area.

### *The Cornwall Railway*

From Plymouth, we follow the Cornish Main Line to Penzance, making a number of diversions along the way to look at some of its branches. Around 80 miles in length, the line, which used to be shared for a short distance by services to Waterloo via Okehampton, runs past the dockyards at Devonport, over the River Tamar into Cornwall via Brunel's Royal Albert Bridge and then weaves its way through the county as shown on the accompanying map. It was mostly built by the Cornwall Railway and opened in 1859–60 as part of its route to Falmouth. The first part, however, was built by the SDR as a branch from its Plymouth Millbay terminus, while west of Truro we join the route of the West Cornwall Railway (WCR), which was opened in full in 1852. The line has many short, sharp gradients and is tightly curved in places, with numerous viaducts being used to carry it over the valleys of the many tidal inlets that are encountered en route.

The first 50 miles or so of the line could have been very different to what was eventually built, however. It was at one point proposed that a train ferry should be used to cross the Hamoaze (the body of water at the mouth of the Tamar). It was also suggested that the line should have passed to the south of Truro and crossed the Penryn River using a drawbridge, but these ideas were rejected by the House of Lords. The idea of a ferry was duly abandoned, with the railway instead crossing the Tamar two miles above Torpoint and then continuing from Saltash along the north bank of the Lynher River to St Germans, from where it loosely follows the route that was originally set out as far as Probus before running around the north side of Truro. The idea of using an atmospheric system, as on the SDR, was also dropped after their shortcomings became apparent.

It was far from plain sailing even when construction eventually got under way. Despite Brunel's plan to use timber trestle viaducts to reduce capital costs, these being significantly cheaper than traditional masonry viaducts, the financial depression that followed the railway mania of the 1840s meant that more cost-cutting measures had to be employed. To further reduce the commitment to shareholders, it was suggested that the line should be built as single track. Even this was not enough, though, and the company's directors had to approach the Associated Companies (a consortium consisting of the B&ER, GWR and SDR) for financial assistance to complete the line, the majority of which was opened in 1859. The line from Truro to Falmouth, which was later relegated to branch line status when through services between Paddington and Penzance were introduced, was eventually opened in 1863.

### *The West Cornwall Railway*

Continuing westwards from Truro, we join the route of the WCR through what used to be the main tin and copper mining area in the county. During the early 19th century, the development of railways facilitated a major expansion of these activities. Most lines were built purely for industrial purposes, but from 1843 the Hayle Railway also carried passengers over its main line between Hayle and Redruth. This was subsequently taken over by the WCR and extensively rebuilt to form part of the line linking Truro with Penzance. Following the opening of the line from Plymouth, this then allowed the residents of west Cornwall to travel to London by rail, albeit the different gauges used meant that passengers had to change trains at Truro. The WCR was originally planned to be built as a broad gauge route, but a shortage of funds meant that it was instead built to standard gauge to avoid the expense of having to rebuild all the existing line. Timber trestle viaducts were again used to minimise the costs of construction. In order to facilitate the operation of through services, the line was rebuilt to mixed gauge in 1866–67. It reverted to standard gauge in 1892 when all the remaining broad gauge lines were done away with.

### *Penzance*

After leaving the central mining district behind, it is not far until Penzance is reached, with the line running along the shore of Mount's Bay for the final few miles from Marazion. Although small in comparison to where we started our journey, the station that serves the historic port features no fewer than four platforms and has a sizeable station building, which is dressed in local granite and has an overall roof covering the west end of the three main platforms. With a small goods yard alongside the station, not to mention further goods handling facilities, carriage sidings and a motive power depot a little way to the east, there was plenty to occupy any rail enthusiasts that visited during the latter days of the steam era. Sadly, like at many of the other locations that we have visited en route, much of this has since been swept away in response to changing demands.

# THE CORNISH MAIN LINE AND ITS CONNECTIONS

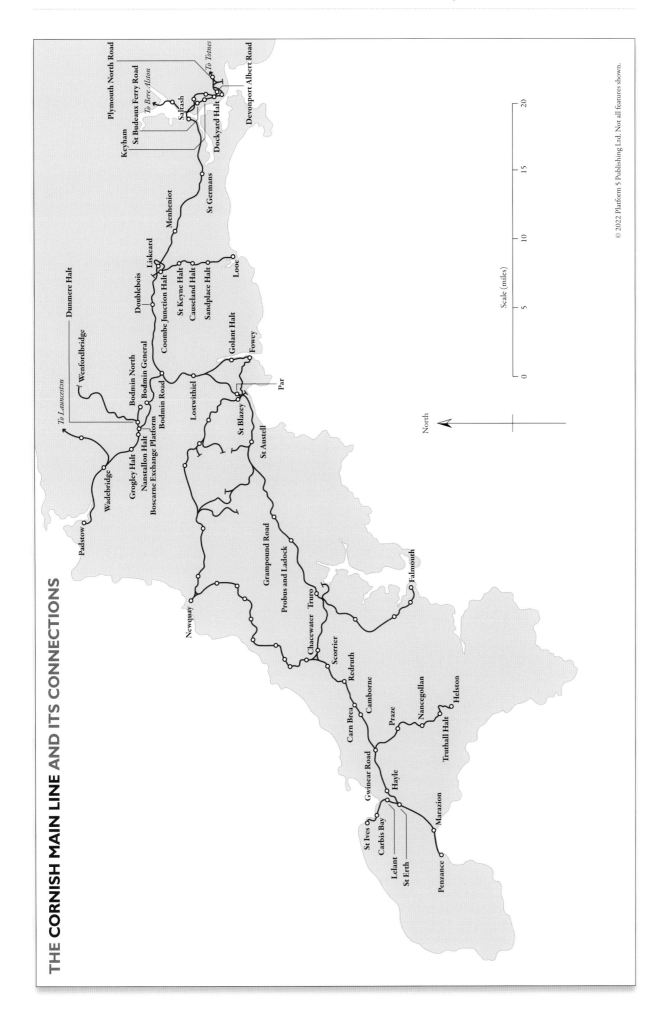

© 2022 Platform 5 Publishing Ltd. Not all features shown.

Scale (miles)

0   5   10   15   20

North

**Right:** Possibly the same locomotive as is illustrated below right, ex-GWR Hawksworth 6400 Class 0-6-0PT No. 6419 arrives at Saltash with an autotrain from Plymouth on 20 September 1959. Built at Swindon Works in December 1934, the locomotive spent much of its life operating out of Laira motive power depot on duties such as this but was transferred away (to Lydney) around a year after this photograph was taken (in August 1960). It ended its career at Yeovil Town, being withdrawn from service in December 1964 and dismantled by John Cashmore Ltd of Newport, Monmouthshire in April 1965. Note the token exchange apparatus to the right of the first coach, onto which locomotive crews were intended to place the token for the single-line section across the Royal Albert Bridge. *Dave Marriot*

**Above:** Ex-GWR Collett 7800 Class 4-6-0 No. 7812 "Erlestoke Manor" and ex-GWR Churchward 4073 Class 4-6-0 No. 5028 "Llantilio Castle" await departure from Plymouth's Platform 7 on 20 September 1959.

Designed as a lighter version of the earlier Collett 6800 Class locomotives for use over branch lines and cross-country routes that these and the Collett 4900 Class 4-6-0s were barred from, the 7800 Class locomotives were no strangers to the South-West but they appear to have evaded Dave during his visits to the area, this being the only photograph that we have so far found in his collection. No. 7812 was, in fact, a local engine, it being based at this time at Plymouth's Laira motive power depot for use on piloting duties over the Devon banks. Displaced as a result of the introduction the new, more powerful diesel-hydraulics and train lengths being reduced, it was transferred to Truro soon afterwards, however. After spending a year there, it ended its days working around Shrewsbury. Withdrawn in November 1965 after the operation of the Cambrian routes was transferred to BR's London Midland Region, which replaced the "Manors" with BR Standards, it was subsequently sold to Woodham Brothers Ltd of Barry. The locomotive was resold into preservation in June 1973 and has since been returned to steam by the Erlestoke Manor Fund.

No. 5028 did not have such a happy ending. Less than three months after this photograph was taken, the locomotive was involved in a collision with "Warship" No. D 602 "Bulldog" at Devonport Junction. Due to a defect in its rear cab, after coming off the 21.50 Paddington–Penzance sleeper service, the North British diesel-hydraulic was sent to turn on the Millbay triangle. Unfortunately, whilst travelling from Devonport Junction to Cornwall Junction, it failed, undetected, across the main line. With the signalman unaware of the blockage, the road was reset and the "Castle", which had taken over from the "Warship" at Plymouth, collided with the defective diesel. The resultant damage to the 4-6-0's front end would probably have been repaired if the incident had occurred earlier on in its life, but because steam traction was beginning to be phased out by then it was taken out of traffic. It was the only member of the Castle Class to be withdrawn as the result of an accident. The "Warship", meanwhile, was admitted to Swindon Works for a Light Casual repair and returned to service in January 1960. *Dave Marriot*

**Below:** An unidentified ex-GWR Hawksworth 6400 Class 0-6-0PT propels an autotrain across Brunel's Royal Albert Bridge on 20 September 1959. One of the most well-known structures on Britain's national rail network, the bridge consists of two bowstring tubular plate girders that are suspended around 100 ft above the River Tamar at high water and 17 conventional plate girder approach spans on either side of the river, seven in Devon and ten in Cornwall. Measuring 455 ft in length, each of the bridge's two main spans is made up of a cast iron segmental tube forming an arch and two pairs of suspension chains hanging on either side in a catenary curve, which counteract the outward thrust that the tube exerts onto the bridge's abutments, with 11 pairs of vertical members restrained with diagonal bracing slung beneath the tube to support the plate girders that carry the single-track railway. Their inner ends are supported by four octagonal columns linked by trelliswork, which are mounted on a single mid-stream pier, while the outer ends rest upon plinths built from granite. Pairs of similar, but less substantial, structures are used to support the approach spans. Officially opened by HRH Prince Albert on 2 May 1859, the bridge was subsequently adorned with the words "I.K. Brunel Engineer 1859" as a memorial to its designer, who died later that year at the age of 53. The structure was granted Grade I listed status in 1952. The scene has since been changed through the construction of a suspension bridge, known as the Tamar Bridge, that carries the A38 trunk road over the river alongside the railway. *Dave Marriot*

**Above:** Ex-GWR Collett 4073 Class 4-6-0 No. 5029 "Nunney Castle" leads 1Z22, the 08.05 Bristol Temple Meads–Par "Cornishman" charter, across the Grade II listed Forder Viaduct on the afternoon of 10 July 2011. Situated around one and a quarter miles west of Saltash in the shadow of Trematon Castle and high above a tidal mill, the structure was built to carry the Cornish Main Line across Forder Lake, a creek leading into the estuary of the Lynher River. It replaced a timber trestle structure, which was at a lower level closer to the river. Between Defiance and St Germans, the original route of the railway followed the Lynher closely and featured no less than six viaducts, all of timber construction. The cost of their maintenance was part of the reasoning behind the GWR's decision to build a new route further to the north. The deviation, four miles and five chains in length, required the construction of new viaducts at Forder, Lynher and St Germans and a tunnel at Wivelscombe. These were completed in time for the new line to be opened in May 1908. Most of the original line was then abandoned and the viaducts were demolished, but at least one short stretch remained in situ (as a siding used for the stabling of coaching stock) until 1964. *Rhys Jones*

**Below:** Having taken over the train from more modern traction at Exeter, ex-GWR Collett 6000 Class 4-6-0 No. 6024 "King Edward I" and ex-GWR Collett 4073 Class 4-6-0 No. 5029 "Nunney Castle" lead Pathfinder Tours' "Eden Limited", 1Z26 05.13 Worcester Shrub Hill–Par, across St Germans Viaduct on the morning of 23 April 2005. In steam days this would have been considered most unusual: the "Kings", which were restricted to double red routes, were too heavy to cross the Royal Albert Bridge and so, officially at least, they were unable to go any further west than Devonport. A number of people claim to have seen members of the class on the opposite side of the Tamar during the days of steam, however. Improvements to the infrastructure over the intervening years mean that there is no such problem nowadays and since becoming the first of the once 30-strong class recorded to have travelled into Cornwall, with the appropriately titled "Par King Pioneer" on 9 May 1998, No. 6024 has visited the Duchy on numerous occasions. The original route of the railway crossed the River Tiddy (at a lower level) just behind the masonry viaduct. *Rhys Jones*

**Right:** Shortly after arriving from Liskeard, ex-GWR Churchward 4500 Class 2-6-2T No. 4569 stands at Looe on 15 June 1960. Before returning, the locomotive and its train would proceed past the photographer to the goods yard for the locomotive to run round. This time-consuming procedure came to an end a little over a year later, however, with DMUs taking over the passenger services along the branch from September 1961. Freight services continued until the goods yard was closed in 1963. The track bed has since been built over. Displaced by dieselisation, the locomotive, meanwhile, was transferred

in July 1961 from St Blazey shed, its home since October 1948, to Whitland. It remained there until April 1963, when it was moved to Westbury. After being placed into store in September that year, it was transferred to Yeovil Town a couple of months later. Its stay there lasted until July 1964. The locomotive was eventually withdrawn from Swindon shed, a stone's throw from where it was built, in August 1964. It was disposed of by the Bird Group at Risca, Newport, Monmouthshire in November 1964. *Dave Marriot*

**Below:** In an almost timeless scene, ex-GWR Collett 4073 Class 4-6-0 No. 5029 "Nunney Castle" leads the return working of The Railway Touring Company's "Cornishman" charter, 1Z24 17.36 Par–Bristol Temple Meads, over East Largin Viaduct on the evening of 10 July 2011. Built to carry Brunel's Cornwall Railway over a deep river valley, the viaduct was rebuilt in 1886, with the piers being raised and lattice girders used to replace the original timber trestles. A number of other viaducts in the county were similarly rebuilt, while others, such as that at Moorswater, were replaced altogether. This allowed the eventual replacement of the single broad gauge line with two standard gauge lines, although in May 1964, with the intention of reducing the load on the structures, the line was once again singled over East Largin and St Pinnock viaducts. Note the three-digit number on the locomotive's smokebox, which was the reporting number given to "The Cornishman" during the summer of 1959. *Rhys Jones*

**Right:** With a maroon-liveried Collett B Set in tow, ex-GWR Churchward 4500 Class 2-6-2T No. 4559 climbs away from Boscarne Junction on the former GWR branch to Bodmin Road on 15 June 1960. The locomotive, which was based at St Blazey motive power depot at this time, was withdrawn just four months later. During its 36 years' service it covered some 915 877 miles. It was scrapped by Woodham Brothers Ltd of Barry in 1961. The line itself had a happier future. Although it lost its passenger services in 1967 and the

decline in freight traffic from Wenfordbridge caused it to be closed in October 1983, it was reopened as far as Boscarne Junction in 1996 by the Bodmin & Wenford Railway. *Dave Marriot*

**Below:** Ex-LSWR Beattie 0298 Class 2-4-0WT No. 30585 arrives at Boscarne Junction with a short freight train on 14 June 1960. Based at nearby Wadebridge, Beattie Well Tanks Nos. 30585–30587 represented the oldest locomotive design still in use by BR at this time, the first of their former classmates having been introduced by the LSWR almost a century earlier. Originally used on suburban services in and around London, the locomotives owed their longevity to the fact that for many years there was nothing else suitable to work the Wenfordbridge branch, which was lightly laid and tightly curved. A trial of an ex-SECR P Class 0-6-0T in 1929 resulted in the track being damaged by its long wheelbase. It was only when a trio of ex-GWR Collett 1366 Class 0-6-0PTs (Nos. 1367–1369) were made redundant at Weymouth in 1962 that the locomotives, which had been much modified by then, with very little left of the originals, were able to be retired. *Dave Marriot*

**Above:** Ex-LSWR Beattie 0298 Class 2-4-0WT No. 30585 hauls a train of empty china clay wagons across Dunmere Junction, where the branches to Bodmin North and Wenfordbridge diverged, on 14 June 1960. Following their closure, the former in January 1967 and the latter in October 1983, the routes became part of the Camel Trail, an approximately 17 mile-long multi-user trail that follows the River Camel from Wenfordbridge to Padstow. *Dave Marriot*

**Below:** A little further on from the last shot at Dunmere Junction, No. 30585 crosses the main road between Bodmin and Wadebridge with a train of empty china clay wagons bound for Wenfordbridge on 15 June 1960. *Dave Marriot*

**Below:** One of the two ex-LSWR Beattie 0298 Class 2-4-0WTs that survive in preservation, No. 30585 heads away from Wadebridge with a short freight train on 13 June 1960. *Dave Marriot*

**Above:** Viewed from the opposite side of the tracks, ex-LSWR Drummond T9 Class 4-4-0 No. 30313 stands at Wadebridge with a North Cornwall Line service towards Exeter on 13 June 1960. Note that although the locomotive, which was built at Nine Elms Works in May 1901, was originally paired with one of the eight-wheeled watercart tenders, so called because they had a tendency to leak and doused the tracks in a similar manner to the vehicles that were used to spray the streets in the late 19th and early 20th centuries, it later acquired a six-wheel tender when it was transferred away from the Western Section of the SR (the watercart tenders were too long for the turntables of the Central and Eastern Sections). As one of the locomotives from the final batch to be built, it also features a wider cab than its older classmates and its splashers extend almost all the way to the edge of the running plates. The locomotive was withdrawn from service at Exmouth Junction motive power depot just over a year after this photograph was taken, in July 1961, and was scrapped at Eastleigh Works only a matter of months later. *Dave Marriot*

**Right:** Framed by the station footbridge, a prefabricated concrete structure typical of BR's Southern Region, ex-LSWR Beattie 0298 Class 2-4-0WT No. 30586 is seen resting alongside Platform 1 at Wadebridge later that same day. The presence of a brake van at the rear of the train may be an indicator that it would soon set off. As well as there being a number of passenger trains to which freight vehicles were regularly added at Wadebridge and the daily trip workings to Wenfordbridge, which left shortly after 10.00 and usually returned at around 16.30, each day there were two freight services that originated at Wadebridge and headed over the North Cornwall Line towards Okehampton. These departed the town at 11.35 and 17.00. The time on the town hall clock suggests that this might have been the first of those two trains. *Dave Marriot*

**Left:** As well as working trains over the Wenfordbridge branch, the Beattie Well Tanks performed station pilot duties at Wadebridge for many years. No. 30586, which was noticeably different from the others in having square splashers, shunts an ensemble of goods vehicles on 13 June 1960, to form the freight service illustrated above. Unfortunately, unlike its sisters, this locomotive was not saved for preservation. Withdrawn in December 1962, it was scrapped at Eastleigh Works in March 1964 having travelled a total of 1 324 050 miles during its 88½ years of service. *Dave Marriot*

**Right:** Ex-LSWR Drummond T9 Class 4-4-0 No. 30338 waits at Wadebridge with a westbound service bound for Padstow on 13 June 1960. Although the locomotive is very much the focus of the photograph, it is worth examining its surroundings. On the left, outside of the engine shed, is an overhead crane. This might seem like an unusual piece of equipment for such a small shed but being well over 100 miles away from Exmouth Junction, the Southern Region's main motive power depot in the West Country, the staff at Wadebridge had to be self-

sufficient. To the right of the locomotive is water column and brazier, which would have been used during the colder months to stop the water supply from freezing up, and in the background there is sign directing station users to a library. *Dave Marriot*

**Below:** The same locomotive as is illustrated above is pictured at Padstow a little later on 13 June 1960. At almost 260 miles from Waterloo, Padstow was the south-westerly outpost of the LSWR and its successor the SR. It was, of course, the terminus of the "Atlantic Coast Express". Note the roof board on the coach to the left of the locomotive. Unfortunately, the users of the "ACE" and the other services along the North Cornwall Line were not numerous enough to warrant its survival. Outside of the summer months passenger numbers were poor and this led the line being listed for closure in Dr Beeching's 1963 report, *The Reshaping of British Railways*. Goods traffic ceased in September 1964, along with most of the through trains to and from Waterloo. All through services were suspended by the end of September 1966, after which Padstow could only be reached by changing trains at Bodmin Road. The line from Wadebridge to Padstow was eventually closed on 30 January 1967, with track lifting taking place shortly afterwards. The track bed is now part of the Camel Trail, although the area around the station is used as car parking. Part of the station platform has since been demolished, but the building itself survives under the ownership of Padstow Town Council. *Dave Marriot*

**Above:** Having been uncoupled from its train and reversed out of the station, No. 30338 stands on the Padstow turntable on 13 June 1960. Situated alongside the Camel Estuary, this was the second turntable to be installed here. The original, which was 50 ft in length and installed in 1900, was replaced in 1947 with a 65 ft example to allow the newly introduced Bulleid Light Pacifics to be turned. *Dave Marriot*

**Below:** Later the same day, No. 30338 accelerates away from Padstow back towards Exeter with a three-coach train including one of the Maunsell P sets, comprising a Brake Third Corridor coach (No. 2831) and a Brake Corridor Composite coach (No. 6586), which for many years formed the mainstay of local services over the North Cornwall Line. The locomotive, which was built at Nine Elms in 1901, would be withdrawn from Exmouth Junction motive power depot in the April of the following year and was cut up only a matter of months later at Eastleigh Works. *Dave Marriot*

**Left:** With only a matter of months to go until it was taken out of service, ex-GWR Collett 1400 Class 0-4-2T No. 1419 rests at Lostwithiel on 14 June 1960. The locomotive, which was the only member of the once 75-strong class to be shedded in Cornwall (at St Blazey) throughout the 1950s, was at this time a regular on the shuttle services to Fowey, although Collett 4575 Class 2-6-2Ts and 6400 Class 0-6-0PTs also appeared on occasions. The locomotive was placed into store in October that year and was eventually withdrawn in April 1961 after 28 years' service. It was cut up at Swindon Works in September 1961, the same month that the Pressed Steel (Class 121) and Gloucester Railway Carriage & Wagon (Class 122) single-car DMUs took over the operation of the passenger services on the branch. These did not last long, however. Poor ridership saw the services withdrawn in January 1965. The small halt at Golant and the station at Fowey were duly closed, but the line remained in situ to provide access for china clay traffic to the jetties at Carne Point. *Dave Marriot*

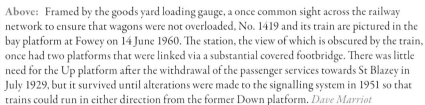

**Above:** Framed by the goods yard loading gauge, a once common sight across the railway network to ensure that wagons were not overloaded, No. 1419 and its train are pictured in the bay platform at Fowey on 14 June 1960. The station, the view of which is obscured by the train, once had two platforms that were linked via a substantial covered footbridge. There was little need for the Up platform after the withdrawal of the passenger services towards St Blazey in July 1929, but it survived until alterations were made to the signalling system in 1951 so that trains could run in either direction from the former Down platform. *Dave Marriot*

**Left:** No. 1419 rolls into the halt at Golant at low tide on 14 June 1960 as a lone passenger waits to board the service to Fowey. *Dave Marriot*

**Above:** Ex-GWR Collett 6000 Class 4-6-0 No. 6024 "King Edward I" and ex-GWR Collett 4073 Class 4-6-0 No. 5029 "Nunney Castle" arrive at Par with Pathfinder Tours' "Eden Limited", 1Z26 05.13 Worcester Shrub Hill–Par, on 23 April 2005. Despite the railways having been much modernised since the end of the steam era, Par is one of several places in Cornwall that are still controlled using traditional semaphore signalling. *Rhys Jones*

**Below:** Ex-GWR Collett 4575 Class 2-6-2T No. 5557 is pictured at Par on 14 June 1960 at the head of what is thought to be a local service for Newquay. The locomotive, which was built at Swindon Works in November 1928, was at this point allocated to the nearby St Blazey shed, along with six classmates – Nos. 4587, 5523, 5534, 5539, 5564 and 5570. It was withdrawn less than six months later, in October 1960, and was disposed of at Swindon in January the following year. *Dave Marriot*

**Above:** With ex-GWR Collett 4575 Class 2-6-2T No. 5557 and its train to Newquay illustrated previously visible on the left, this wider shot also shows the signal box situated at the southern end of Par's Platform 2. Built to a GWR Type 2 design, the box was opened in 1879. Originally, it contained 26 levers and was just 17 ft 8 in long. To cope with increasing volumes of traffic, the structure was extended to more than double its original length in 1893 to accommodate a larger lever frame, which was itself replaced in 1913 with a GWR example made up of 57 levers. Although it has been modified over the intervening years, the box was given a Grade II listing in April 2013 on account of it being one of only two examples of its type to remain in its original location. *Dave Marriot*

**Below:** No. 3635, one of Collett's ubiquitous 5700 Class 0-6-0PTs, leads a local service away from Par and around the sharp curve towards St Blazey on 14 June 1960. Developed from the earlier Dean 2721 Class 0-6-0PTs, the 5700 Class locomotives were the GWR's most numerous design, with a total of 863 being built. Such was their success that production continued until 1950 and a number of locomotives saw service beyond the end of BR steam with both London Transport and the National Coal Board. No. 3635, however, was withdrawn in April 1965 and was scrapped soon afterwards (in August that year) by the Bird Group at Tremains Yard in Bridgend, South Wales. It had a service life of just over 25 years. *Dave Marriot*

**Left:** Ex-GWR Collett 5700 Class 0-6-0PT No. 8719, one of the 25 members of the class that were built by Beyer, Peacock & Co in Manchester in 1931, is pictured approaching St Blazey on 14 June 1960 with a short freight train made up of box vans, likely to be loaded with bagged clay, and mineral wagons, which would have been used to deliver coal to the clay dries at Par Harbour. The roof of Par Bridge signal box, which controlled traffic to and from the nearby harbour and also along the line to Fowey, can just been seen above the fourth and fifth vans in the train. This was closed, along with the former Cornwall Minerals Railway route to Fowey, in October 1968. Immediately afterwards, the route was converted into a private haul road for English China Clays to move china clay from the dries at Par to the deep-water docks at Fowey. No. 8719, meanwhile, was withdrawn from St Blazey shed in May 1962 and was disposed of in November that year by John Cashmore Ltd of Newport, Monmouthshire. *Dave Marriot*

**Above:** Ex-GWR Collett 6800 Class 4-6-0 No. 6825 "Llanvair Grange" leads an eastbound express down the gradient into Par on 14 June 1960.

Often used to assist heavy trains over the Devon banks, the "Granges" were built in the 1930s to replace Churchward's 4300 Class 2-6-0s, the older examples of which were by then becoming worn out. The demand for what was effectively a small-wheeled Collett 4900 Class was recognised long before this, though. In 1901, Churchward put forward the idea of a 4-6-0 with 5 ft 8 in driving wheels and a standard Swindon No. 1 boiler. Collett revived this proposal but modified the design to include a more modern cab and controls. Between 1936 and 1939, 80 4300s were replaced by 6800s, their wheels, motion and tenders being reused by the new locomotives. A further 20 4300s were similarly replaced by the lighter Collett 7800 Class 4-6-0s, which were intended for use on cross-country and branch line duties. Had World War II not intervened, all the remaining 4300s would also have been replaced in this way.

Taking its name from an 18th century country house at Nant-y-derry in Monmouthshire, No. 6825 was built as part of the first batch of the locomotives (Lot No. 308) and entered service in February 1937. Until it was transferred to Laira in July 1962, the entirety of the locomotive's BR career was spent in Cornwall, mostly at Penzance (it was allocated to St Blazey between September 1960 and October 1961). After spells at Reading (from September 1962 to April 1964) and St Philip's Marsh (from April to June 1964), the locomotive was withdrawn from service and it was eventually despatched to the Bird Group's scrapyard at Risca, Newport, Monmouthshire for disposal, which came in December of that year. Although at least a couple of examples were offered to preservationists, none of the class survived. *Dave Marriot*

**Left:** Now looking in the opposite direction, ex-GWR Collett 5101 Class 2-6-2T No. 5198 is pictured as it climbs away from Par with a westbound stopping service on 14 June 1960. One of a total of 140 such locomotives built between 1929 and 1949 to operate local and suburban services across the Great Western network, No. 5198 was outshopped from Swindon in November 1934. It was for many years based in the West Midlands, later having spells at Gloucester and Oxford before being transferred to St Blazey in June 1960. Its stay in Cornwall was a brief one. In October 1960, it was moved to Whitland. It stayed there until it was transferred to Taunton in December 1960, eventually being withdrawn from service in June 1961 and dismantled at Swindon Works in December that year. *Dave Marriot*

**Above:** Ex-GWR Collett 4900 Class 4-6-0 No. 4967 "Shirenewton Hall" leads a westbound train out of Highertown Tunnel, Truro towards the divergence of the Falmouth branch and the main line to Penzance at Penwithers Junction on 16 June 1960. Named after a country house and estate (originally Shirenewton Court) in Monmouthshire, the locomotive was outshopped from the GWR's Swindon Works in December 1929 and was at the time of this photograph being taken allocated to Plymouth's Laira motive power depot. Following a transfer to Exeter and then a spell in storage, it was withdrawn from service at Neath in September 1962 and scrapped by R S Hayes Ltd at Tremains Yard in Bridgend during November 1963. *Dave Marriot*

**Above:** With the River Hayle visible in the background draining into St Ives Bay, and Hayle Power Station to the right, ex-GWR Churchward 4500 Class 2-6-2T No. 4570 approaches Carbis Bay on 13 June 1960. The 4500s were for many years a regular sight on the St Ives branch, first appearing here in the 1920s. Introduced in response to increasing traffic levels and a shortage of other suitable locomotives, they had to be given special authorisation to work over the lightly laid branch, which had an "uncoloured" route classification, meaning that locomotives with an axle loading of over 14.2 tons should have been barred. As can be seen on the locomotive's bunker, the 4500s had a yellow route restriction. By 1961, the locomotives were becoming worn out, which led to the line being dieselised the following year, with the heavier Collett 4575 Class 2-6-2Ts being brought in to work trains over the Helston branch. Apart from the last six months or so, No. 4570 was based in Cornwall for the entirety of its BR career. At the time of this photograph being taken it was shedded at Penzance. It eventually left the county in June 1962 and was transferred to Laira motive power depot, from where it was withdrawn in January 1963. It was scrapped by John Cashmore Ltd of Newport, Monmouthshire in June 1964. *Dave Marriot*

**Left:** A busy scene at Gwinear Road on 17 June 1960. On the right, ex-GWR Churchward 4500 Class 2-6-2T No. 4574 stands at the head of a mixed train from Helston, while ex-GWR Collett 6800 Class 4-6-0 No. 6869 "Resolven Grange" rolls in on the left with a westbound express. As was the case across much of the country at this time, the scene would change significantly within just a matter of years, with almost everything in shot being lost. Apart from the introduction of the North British diesel-hydraulics, relatively little was done to reduce the costs of operating the Helston branch, prompting its passenger services to be withdrawn on 3 November 1962. Ironically, it was the GWR's introduction in 1903 of a connecting motor bus service between Helston, Mullion and The Lizard, the first such service in the world, that helped to bring about the line's eventual demise. Freight services continued until 5 October 1964, when Gwinear Road itself was closed. After almost 40 years' service, the "Small Prairie" was withdrawn around the start of 1963. It was scrapped by John Cashmore Ltd of Newport, Monmouthshire in June 1964. The "Grange", meanwhile, was taken out of service at Cardiff East Dock in July 1965 and was scrapped by the Bird Group at Morriston, Swansea in November that year. It had an operational life of only 26 years. *Dave Marriot*

**Below:** Ex-GWR Collett 4073 Class 4-6-0s Nos. 5029 "Nunney Castle" and 5051 "Earl Bathurst" pass the remains of Marazion station on the afternoon of 31 May 2004 with 1Z28, the 14.10 charter train from Penzance to Ealing Broadway, which was organised by Pathfinder Tours and ran under the title of "The Cornubian". The pair worked the train as far as Exeter St Davids, with the remainder of the journey being diesel hauled. It would reach its destination in the early hours of the following morning!

Situated around two miles out of Penzance, Marazion station was opened by the WCR in March 1852. It was never particularly busy, however. According to BR's Spotlight on Marazion, during the 1950s it enjoyed around 5000 passengers, 44000 parcels (34000 outwards and 10000 inwards) and generated enough freight, mainly broccolli and potatoes, to fill 3000 wagons each year. It was consequently closed during the 1960s, firstly to passengers in October 1964 and to goods traffic in December 1965. Interestingly, its closure required certain bus services between Penzance and Camborne to be diverted to call at the station in the morning and afternoon. Such little use was made of these, though, that in September 1965 the Minister of Transport relaxed this requirement of the BR Board.

The station platforms and most of the buildings, including the signal box that stood on the Down platform, were subsequently demolished, while the sidings that once stood in the vicinity of station were taken up. An isolated stretch of track was, however, left for the stabling of a number of Pullman cars that had been converted into camping coaches, most of which remained in situ, albeit out of use and in increasingly poor condition, until 2003. *Rhys Jones*

**Above:** In what is believed to be a scene from the early 1950s, BR Standard Class 7MT 4-6-2 No. 70024 "Vulcan" blows off steam as it stands underneath the trainshed at Penzance after arriving on the "Cornish Riviera".

One of five such locomotives that were allocated to Plymouth's Laira motive power depot, No. 70024 would have been a reasonably common sight at Penzance between February 1952 and December 1956, but there are a few features that help to date the photograph. As built, the locomotive had hollow axles; however, these were found to cause serious problems. The driving wheels on a lot of the early "Britannias" shifted on their axles, causing the coupling rods to fail. Indeed, No. 70024 had barely travelled 2000 miles before it had to be sent to Swindon Works for modifications to be carried out, which also saw its front coupling rods replaced with plain ones, which were heavier and stronger than the original fluted type. The locomotive made another visit to Swindon in 1954, this time for the fitting of a large dome atop of the water scoop on the tender, raised lids on the sandboxes and a support bracket for the forward regulator rod. As there is no evidence of the sandbox lids, which were originally flush with the locomotive's running plates, it can be deduced that the photograph predates that second visit to Swindon.

Although the "Britannias" were not overly popular with the footplate crews on the Western Region, as their left-hand driving position was contrary to tradition – making the sighting of some signals difficult for their drivers, No. 70024 remained allocated to the Western Region until September 1961. It was then transferred to the London Midland Region and was eventually withdrawn from Carlisle Upperby motive power depot in December 1967. The locomotive was scrapped in April 1968 by Thomas W Ward Ltd at Killamarsh, Derbyshire. *David Wilshaw collection*

# ■ ABBREVIATIONS AND GLOSSARY

## *Abbreviations*

Where a railway company that is referred to regularly is first mentioned in the text of this book, its name is written out in full, followed by its abbreviated form in brackets. The abbreviation is then used where any subsequent references to the company are made. All of the abbreviations used within this publication are listed below:

BR – British Railways
B&ER - Bristol & Exeter Railway
EKR – East Kent Railway
GWR – Great Western Railway
LBSCR – London, Brighton & South Coast Railway
LNER – London & North Eastern Railway
LMS – London, Midland & Scottish Railway
LSWR – London & South Western Railway
RAF - Royal Air Force

RCTS – Railway Correspondence & Travel Society
S&DJR – Somerset & Dorset Joint Railway
S&YR – Salisbury & Yeovil Railway
SDR – South Devon Railway
SECR – South Eastern & Chatham Railway
SR – Southern Railway
WCR – West Cornwall Railway
WD – War Department
WS&WR – Wiltshire, Somerset & Weymouth Railway

**Above:** Ex-SR Maunsell U Class 2-6-0 No. 31639 leads a loaded ballast train near Woking on 3 June 1966. The locomotive, which was outshopped from Ashford Works in May 1931 and entered service as No. A639, was at this point allocated to the nearby Guildford motive power depot. It was withdrawn from service a matter of days later and was dismantled by John Cashmore Ltd of Newport, Monmouthshire during September 1966. *Dave Marriot*

**Above:** Bulleid Battle of Britain Class 4-6-2 No. 34064 "Fighter Command" passes Fleet with a Bournemouth-bound express on 30 April 1966. *Dave Marriot*

## *Glossary*

*Atlantic* - A locomotive that under the Whyte notation has a 4-4-2 wheel arrangement i.e. four leading wheels – two on each axle, four coupled driving wheels and two trailing wheels.

*Atmospheric Railway* - A type of railway that instead of mobile power generating equipment uses differential air pressure to provide propulsion to rail vehicles. In the case of the SDR system, this was achieved using steam-driven pumping stations situated roughly every three miles along the line to create a partial vacuum in a series of slotted tubes located between the rails. Beneath the leading vehicle of each train there was a piston, to which it was attached using an arm that projected through the slot at the top of the tubes. The piston would be inserted into the tube from the end at which the air had been evacuated and, once its brakes were released, atmospheric pressure acting on the piston would propel the train along. With static machinery offering better fuel efficiency, the elimination of heavy locomotives meaning that lighter track materials could be used, and the availability of greater power allowing trains to negotiate steeper than usual gradients, proponents claimed the atmospheric system offered significant savings when it came to the construction and operating costs. Not only this, the system was said to improve safety by removing the risk of collisions, preventing derailments and removing the very real risk to passengers of a boiler explosion.

*AWS (Automatic Warning System)* - A safety system introduced by BR during the 1950s to provide train drivers with both an audible warning and a visual reminder that they were approaching either a distant signal set at caution or a home signal set at danger (or,

in the case of colour light signals, a double yellow, yellow or red aspect) and that they would have to take action as appropriate. If the warnings went unacknowledged within the required time frame, the system would automatically apply a train's emergency brakes to bring it safely to a stand.

*Broad Gauge* - A term used to describe railway lines where, in an effort to enable to trains to operate at greater speeds and also improve the level of comfort for passengers, the inner heads of the two rails are set further apart than the 4 ft 8½ in of standard gauge lines. Within Great Britain, broad gauge is generally considered to mean a gauge of 7 ft ¼ in, as was used by Isambard Kingdom Brunel during the construction of much of the GWR network. Upon the recommendation of Parliament's Gauge Commission, which favoured what become known as standard gauge, broad gauge tracks were restricted to the South-West of England and Wales, which led to them gradually being replaced to avoid operational problems, with the main line from Exeter to Truro and various connecting branches being rebuilt as a standard gauge during the final push over the weekend of 21–22 May 1892.

*Bunker* - The area to the rear of the cab on a tank engine where its coal supplies are usually located.

*Diesel-Hydraulic Locomotive* - A diesel locomotive with a hydraulic (rather than an electric or a mechanical) transmission. Such locomotives were once common on BR's Western Region, the management of which believed that lightweight diesel-hydraulic locomotives with stressed-steel skins, similar to those that were

WATERLOO TO THE **WEST COUNTRY**

introduced by the German Federal Railways in the early 1950s, would be cheaper to construct and would be capable of hauling heavier trains than comparable diesel-electric locomotives.

*DMU (Diesel Multiple Unit)* - A self-contained passenger train, often made up of two or three vehicles, with underfloor diesel engines and driving cabs at the outer ends, which became common in Britain during the 1950s and 1960s as the management of the railways strived to cut costs. Provided that they are compatible, multiple units can be combined to form longer trains to meet passenger demand and enable trains to split and join en route without the need for complicated shunting manoeuvres as would be the case with a locomotive-hauled train. Another advantage is that their multiple engines mean that the units are not as vulnerable to failures as a traditional locomotive-hauled train would be.

*EMU (Electric Multiple Unit)* - A self-contained passenger train similar to a DMU but propelled by an external electric source, usually a lineside conductor rail or an overhead supply, powering its on-board traction motors.

*Grouping* - The reorganisation of the railway system in Great Britain under the 1921 Railways (Grouping) Act, which was intended to make the railways more efficient and reduce losses by consolidating 120 railway companies into what became known as "the Big Four", which was made up of the GWR, LNER, LMS and SR.

*Hammer Blow* - A vertical force caused by a steam locomotive's driving wheels being unbalanced in order to offset horizontal reciprocating masses, such as valve gear components, to improve its ride, which is transferred to the track through the driving wheels.

*Light Pacific* - A type of locomotive comprising both the Battle of Britain and West Country Class 4-6-2s that was designed by Bulleid as a smaller version of the earlier Merchant Navy Class locomotives with an 18 ton axle loading and 8 ft 6 in wide cabs (as built) for use almost across the full length and breadth of the SR network.

*Locomotive Exchanges* - A series of trials organised by the newly formed BR in 1948, which took place over a period of five months (mid-April to the end of August that year) and involved a variety of locomotives, including express, mixed-traffic and freight engines, being exchanged between the regions that replaced the four companies that had operated Britain's main line railways since the Grouping in 1923 (the GWR, LNER, LMS and SR) to thoroughly evaluate their different designs, with the intention that the best ideas from the different locomotive designers involved would be incorporated into the new BR Standard designs.

*Mixed Gauge* - A way of describing a railway line capable of carrying rolling stock of multiple gauges, which often share a common rail. In Great Britain, mixed gauge tracks were often found where broad gauge and standard gauge lines met.

*Mogul* - A locomotive that under the Whyte notation has a 2-6-0 wheel arrangement i.e. two leading wheels – one on each axle, six coupled driving wheels and no trailing wheels.

*Pacific* - A locomotive that under the Whyte notation has a 4-6-2 wheel arrangement i.e. four leading wheels – two on each axle, six coupled driving wheels and two trailing wheels.

*Prairie* - A locomotive that under the Whyte notation has a 2-6-2 wheel arrangement i.e. two leading wheels – two on each axle, six coupled driving wheels and two trailing wheels.

*Running Powers* - An agreement allowing one railway company to run trains over the lines of another.

*Shed* - An abbreviation of engine shed, both of which were commonly used to refer to motive power depots during the steam era.

*Smokebox* - Appearing as a forward extension of a steam locomotive's boiler barrel, mounted on a saddle bolted to the locomotive's main frames, this is where steam from the cylinders and exhaust gases from the firebox come together to escape via the chimney.

*Splashers* - The pieces of metalwork that cover the top of steam locomotives' driving wheels where they protrude through the running plate – the narrow walkways usually found on either side of a locomotive's boiler.

*Standard Gauge* - A phrase used to describe railway lines where the inner heads of the two rails are positioned a distance of 4 ft 8½ in apart, as was used by railway pioneer George Stephenson when he and later his son, Robert, were employed to engineer a number of railway lines, including the Stockton & Darlington Railway, the world's first railway to operate both freight and public passenger services using steam traction, and the Liverpool & Manchester Railway, the world's first inter-city railway line. The gauge was chosen so that the hundreds of horse-drawn chaldron wagons found in the collieries in the North of England could operate on the Stockton & Darlington line without having to be modified. It became so widespread that by the time of the Railway Regulation (Gauge) Act, which saw 4 ft 8½ in become the standard gauge of railway lines within Great Britain, was passed in August 1846 there were eight times as many miles of 4 ft 8½ in gauge line in the country as there were of 7 ft ¼ in gauge.

*Station Pilot* - A locomotive that is based at a principal station to perform shunting duties.

*Superheater* - A device fitted inside the boilers of some steam locomotives to increase their power output (and improve efficiency) to enable heavier trains to be hauled at higher speeds by taking saturated steam from the main steam pipe and passing it through superheater elements (small-diameter tubes within the large-diameter boiler tubes) to raise its temperature to the point that any moisture present would be converted into additional steam.

*Tractive Effort* - A term used to describe the force that can be generated by a locomotive for moving a train.

*Up/Down Line* - In order to help describe the exact location of a train or an item of railway infrastructure on Britain's rail network, railway lines are usually referred to as running either in the Up or Down direction, with individual tracks being given names such as Up Fast, Up Slow, Down Fast or Down Slow, these names often giving an indication of their usage. Generally, an Up line leads towards the location in which the railway that built the line was headquartered, which in the case of English railway companies was often London, although there were some exceptions to this.

*Water Troughs* - Long troughs, filled with water that lay between the rails on level sections of track, which allowed locomotives' water supplies to be replenished on the move using a water scoop, a device that could be lowered into the troughs when travelling at speed to direct the water into locomotives' tenders or tanks.

*Whyte Notation* - A method of classifying steam (and some diesel and electric) locomotives according to their wheel arrangement introduced in the early 20th century, with the number of leading (non-driving) wheels, the number of coupled driving wheels and the number of trailing (non-driving) wheels separated by dashes. For example, a locomotive with four leading wheels (two on each axle), six coupled driving wheels and two trailing wheels would be described as a 4-6-2. A T suffix indicates a steam locomotive fitted with side tanks; ST a saddle tank; PT a pannier tank; and WT a well tank.

*Withered Arm* - An unofficial name that was given to the former LSWR lines to the west of Exeter.

**Above:** Rebuilt Bulleid Merchant Navy Class 4-6-2 No. 35030 "Elder-Dempster Lines" races through Hook with an express service from Bournemouth to Waterloo on 29 July 1966. The last one of the locomotives to be built under Order No. 3393, No. 35030 was outshopped from Eastleigh Works in April 1949 and entered service (at Bournemouth) wearing malachite green livery. After being transferred to Dover in October 1949 and repainted into BR express blue livery in May 1950, it was named "Elder-Dempster Lines" at Southampton Docks on 5 June 1950 by Mr G H Avezathe, who was then the Director of the shipping line after which it was named. A further repaint (into BR green) came in May 1953 and in June 1955 the locomotive was transferred to Nine Elms motive power depot to work services over the South West Main Line from Waterloo. Having covered 351 234 miles in its original air-smoothed form, it was rebuilt at Eastleigh Works in April 1958. Based at Weymouth from September 1964 to April 1967, the locomotive ended its days at Nine Elms and, with a total mileage of 850 876, was withdrawn from service immediately after working the 14.07 Weymouth–Waterloo on 9 July 1967. *Dave Marriot*

**Above:** Named after a senior British Army officer who served in both World Wars and acted as General Officer Commanding-in-Chief of Anti-Aircraft Command throughout World War II – the only British General to hold the same position throughout the conflict, rebuilt Bulleid Battle of Britain Class 4-6-2 No. 34058 "Sir Frederick Pile" accelerates an inter-regional service away from Basingstoke in October 1964. An unidentified Light Pacific stands alongside. *Dave Marriot*

**Above:** On the afternoon of 21 August 2004, ex-GWR Collett 4073 Class 4-6-0s Nos. 5029 "Nunney Castle" and 5051 "Earl Bathurst" climb the 1-in-42 gradient of Hemerdon bank with the return working of Past Time Rail's "Devonian" railtour, 1Z31 16.40 Plymouth–Reading, which they would work as far as Bristol Temple Meads. *Rhys Jones*